Waxahachie

Where Cotton Reigned King

Waxahachians led an active social life. Parades were a frequent occurrence in the city and local women decked out their carriage for this one.

THE
MAKING OF AMERICA
SERIES

WAXAHACHIE

WHERE COTTON REIGNED KING

KELLY MCMICHAEL STOTT

ARCADIA
PUBLISHING

ISBN 978-0-7385-2389-7

Published by Arcadia Publishing,
Charleston SC, Chicago IL, Portsmouth NH, San Francisco CA

Printed in the United States

Library of Congress control number: 2002107475

For all general information contact Arcadia Publishing at:
Telephone 843-853-2070
Fax 843-853-0044
E-Mail sales@arcadiapublishing.com
For customer service and orders:
Toll-Free 1-888-313-2665

Visit us on the Internet at www.arcadiapublishing.com

FRONT COVER: *Throughout the trying years of World War II, Waxahachie's downtown square remained the heart of the city. Citizens gathered to mourn their dead and celebrate their living. Although the cars and clothing look different today, the "square" is still a favorite gathering place for locals.*

CONTENTS

ACKNOWLEDGMENTS

Several years ago while I was still in the midst of my doctoral degree, I was driving west on Main Street in Waxahachie when I thought how nice it would be to write a book about the community, but of course I knew this would have to wait until I was a tenured professor with lots of time and departmental funding (how naïve I was back then!). So I would like to thank my editor, Christine T. Riley at Arcadia Publishing. She was almost as excited as I was about this project, despite the fact that I was just a lowly adjunct professor.

I owe a large debt of gratitude to Shannon Simpson at the Ellis County Museum, who provided helpful insights to sources and pointed the way to finding the many wonderful pictures included in this book. The librarians at Nicholas P. Sims Library were always helpful, although I do not think they understood my sudden interest in all things Waxahachie. I have been patronizing that library since I was old enough to urge my mother to drive me there from my home in the neighboring town of Midlothian. I would also like to say thank you to the many individuals who shared stories about growing up in Waxahachie or their personal research into the community's history, especially Mrs. Barnwell, Chief David Hughes, and Kirk Hunter. As always, thanks to my mentors, Dr. Richard Lowe, Dr. Mike Campbell, and Dr. Rebecca Sharpless, who always respond to my emails.

I also appreciate my departmental head at Texas Christian University, Dr. Clayton Brown, for offering me the opportunity to teach at TCU and opening the university's many resources to my disposal. Dr. Brown's keen interest in the project (he spent summers in Waxahachie with his grandparents) and willingness to reminisce opened up new avenues of research and inquiry.

Most of all, I would like to say thank you to my family. My husband Ian, who has continued to support me through too many ventures, and my children Ryan and Emma, who are eternally grateful that this project did not require too many long drives for research. Thanks to my brother Kyle, who put up with my constant babbling about all the fascinating things I was discovering and even tried to help find sources, and to my brother Justin and his family, Heather and Hannah, who encouraged me and remained curious. Finally, a big thank you to my mom and dad. I appreciate the roots you planted for me in one small Texas town and the wings you offered so that I could fly high enough to appreciate the part my family played in the making of Waxahachie and Ellis County.

This photograph shows the christening of the S.S. Waxahachie *in 1919, a merchant ship named in honor of the "queen city of the cotton belt." Waxahachie contributed so greatly to the World War I effort that this merchant ship was named after the community. The S.S.* Waxahachie *plied the world's oceans for many years.*

INTRODUCTION

Excitement filled the air in Waxahachie, Texas on the morning of October 29, 1902. Dogs yelped at the clouds of dust being stirred up, children pushed and elbowed to get closer to the road's edge, and even the adults leaned and stretched over their childrens' heads for the chance to see Buffalo Bill and his Wild West Show. William F. Cody and his troupe had rolled into town the previous day—49 railroad cars had been needed to transport the more than 1,200 men, women, horses, and buffalo that were parading around the courthouse square. The pageantry advertised the show's afternoon and evening performances, but the local people needed no encouragement. Families gathered from throughout the county to take in the production and to visit with neighbors and friends. The people laughed and joked throughout the day, and relaxed as the past few months' strenuous labor to harvest and gin the cotton crop began to fade from memory. Many of the old-timers related tales of the pioneer days of the county, their memories sparked during the matinee when actors dressed as cowboys chased buffalo around the arena and squared off against costumed Indians. Some of these men laughingly claimed that it was not so long ago that Waxahachie had been part of this "Old West."

For over 150 years, Waxahachie has geographically and figuratively been the heart of Ellis County. Drawn originally by the gently rolling hills, abundant natural springs, and highly fertile soils, settlers found the climate healthy and the local Native Americans friendly. Most stayed and spent their lives creating a community that led the state and, at times, the nation in agricultural production—particularly in the growing of cotton. For a period of more than 20 years, Ellis reigned as the top cotton-producing county in the nation, and Waxahachie reflected the wealth that accompanied "king cotton."

The city prospered after the Civil War and Reconstruction—in large part due to the flood of immigrants from the old southern and border states that began to arrive in the county in 1873 and who, while looking for fertile soil, brought cotton culture to the blackland prairie. The emphasis on this single cash crop created a booming economy, and local businessmen and planters created a thriving downtown sector, initiated the electrification of the city, and built ornately decorated Victorian and gingerbread–style mansions. As the community continued

One of the treats of the 1930s and 1940s, Waxahachie's soda fountain was popular with the young and old. Offering specialties like the "brown cow," a mixture of vanilla ice cream, chocolate syrup, and root beer, soda fountains were a mainstay of social life.

to prosper, town leaders created an interurban electric railway system that linked Waxahachie with Dallas to the north and Waco to the south, and persuaded Trinity University to relocate. Trinity, which provided higher education to whites in the north-central Texas area, combined with Oak Lawn Academy, one of the few accredited quality centers of education available to African-American central Texans, helped to make Waxahachie a center for learning and cultural uplift in the region, a role made more obvious when the Texas Synod of the Cumberland Presbyterian Church located their annual Chautauqua Summer Assembly permanently in the city.

By the 1930s, the community, along with most of the nation, began to falter. Waxahachie's reliance on cotton as the root of its prosperity had led to untold wealth for the city and a great many citizens, but when the markets collapsed during the Great Depression, the county's farmers were devastated and all the community's industry—consisting overwhelmingly of cotton gins, compresses, and a textile mill—crumbled. The people of Waxahachie struggled through the Depression years. Many simply left for larger urban areas to seek work in one of President Roosevelt's New Deal programs. Those who stayed behind tried to pick up the pieces after the Depression and World War II. They realized that for the city to regain its place of prominence among Texas towns, they would have to diversify the economy.

Today, Waxahachie enjoys a balanced economy between varied manufacturing, agribusiness, and commerce. The boom-then-bust cycle that plagued the community in the early part of the twentieth century has left the city's greatest historical treasures intact. Its stately courthouse, designed by James Reily Gordon in 1895, is the city's most commanding landmark. At the same time, multiple streets are lined with pristine older homes and the Chautauqua Auditorium in Getzendaner Park still opens its doors after a hundred years to cultural venues. Dozens of clubs and organizations provide the town's citizens with a variety of social and intellectual activities, a university and a community college have made Waxahachie their home, and tourists flock to the city, especially during the summer when the local historical society hosts an annual tour of homes and thousands of crepe myrtles are in bloom. Visitors come to see the stately mansions, eat in the fine restaurants, shop on the square, and visually remember what life was like when cotton reigned king in Waxahachie.

An early street scene, Waxahachians met on the downtown square for many different social events. In this picture taken in 1902, the community gathered to see the parade kicking off the arrival of Ringling Brothers Circus to the town. Notice the onlookers on the second- and third-floor balconies of the courthouse, areas no longer accessible to the public.

1. The Prairies Were Alive with Buffalo

John Billingsley stepped out of the makeshift shelter he had helped his parents construct the week before. He looked back at the structure, not fancy enough to even be called a cabin. The family had made the three-sided dwelling of logs found in the nearby creek bottoms and it remained opened on the south side to catch the afternoon breeze. John's mother and sister had chinked the holes between the logs of the three walls with prairie grass and mud, and swept the dirt floor clean. When they were finished, John's father had removed the canvas cover from the wagon, draped it across the top of the logs to form a roof, then weighed it down with more logs.

As sparse as the shelter seemed, the family was glad to have it. For almost six months, the Billingsley family had traveled from Missouri in a covered wagon. Most nights, the men had slept on the ground under the wagon while the women slept inside or stretched canvas to form tents. Breaking camp and moving on a daily basis had taken its toll. John sensed his parent's excitement, though, when they crossed the Red River and were at last in Texas. A carpet of green grass lay in front of them. The rolling prairies teemed with wild antelope, deer, horses, hens, and turkeys, and John's father claimed that there was no limit to what a man could do with such land.

The Billingsleys, like the hundreds of other families who traveled to north-central Texas in the mid-1840s, came in search of fertile, cheap land and a new start. These Americans, most from Tennessee and Missouri, began immigrating to the state in large numbers shortly after Texas declared itself an independent republic and won its war against Mexico. By the time Texans voted to join the Union in 1845, the state was attracting an increasing number of pioneers each year. These new citizens joined earlier settlers, many of whom had arrived as early as the 1820s to claim land grants from first the Spanish and then the Mexican governments. But not all of Texas's inhabitants were Anglo; the state had a large indigenous population that was often in conflict with the American pioneers.

No Native Americans lived permanently in the region that later became known as Ellis County. Nevertheless, many different tribes traveled through the area to hunt the abundant wildlife and camp along the many creeks and springs. Most of these natives belonged to a band known as the Tonkawa, derived from the Waco word *tonkawya*, meaning "they all stay together." The Tonkawa called themselves *tichkan-watich*, or "the most human of peoples," and consisted of several different groups who came together in the early eighteenth century to try and survive. A matrilineal clan, the Tonkawa practiced Plains culture following and living off the buffalo and other small game. Though some had attempted farming, they were not successful and remained a nomadic people.

Anglos living in Texas were attracted to the Tonkawa and repelled by them at the same time. Generally a peaceful people, the tribe often camped near pioneer settlements and bartered for provisions with whites. The Tonkawa signed a treaty of peace and commercial alliance with United States officials at Council Spring along the Brazos River in Robertson County in 1846. Now allied with the Texans, the Tonkawa fought with the Anglo settlers when the Comanches and Apaches went on the warpath. Continuing this alliance, tribal men served throughout the late 1840s and 1850s as scouts for the Texas Rangers and the United States Army. Despite these associations and gestures of good will, there was much about Tonkawa tribal life that Texans simply could not understand or accept.

The Texans and Tonkawa could not cross the gulf of their cultural barrier. For example, settlers in the Ellis County area never reconciled to seeing the scantily dressed tribal peoples crossing their lands. The men wore long breechcloths and adorned their faces and chests with tattoos and jewelry they had fashioned from bones, shells, and feathers. The women wore only short skirts, leaving their breasts bare, which they highlighted with tattooed concentric circles around the nipples. The children went entirely nude—repugnant enough to many "well brought up" southern women—but these ladies found the Tonkawa practice of binding boards to the newborn Native American babies' heads deplorable and inhumane, and could never understand why the tribe found flattened foreheads attractive. Despite their differences, however, the Tonkawa had always been friendly with the Americans living along Waxahachie Creek and both groups lived in relative peace.

By the late 1840s, having been pushed off their traditional lands by the Apaches and hemmed in by new Anglo settlements, the Tonkawa faced starvation. The dwindling number of buffalo had greatly reduced their food supply and the tribe began to scavenge to subsist. In addition to the small mammals they captured, the Tonkawa ate fish and oysters from fresh water streams and harvested wild herbs, roots, seeds, fruits, and nuts. Still, the Tonkawa needed help to survive.

The immediate needs of the Tonkawa coincided perfectly with the country's policy on Native Americans. The starving tribe was easily persuaded to leave its hunting area (including what would become Ellis County) and move to a reservation with the Caddo and Anadarko along the Brazos River in Young County in 1855. Displaced again in 1859 by encroaching Anglos, the Tonkawa were relocated to the Washita River in Oklahoma. Two years later, hoping to improve their declining condition, the tribe allied with the Confederacy during the Civil War and served as scouts in the Trans-Mississippi Department. The next year, while the remaining young men of the tribe were fighting for the South, the

Delaware, Shawnee, and Caddo tribes united, attacked, and killed 133 Tonkawa. Less than 200 of the band remained, wandered back into Texas—hoping to flee the tribes that had attacked them—and fell into stealing to survive. Plagued by alcohol problems and starvation, the Tonkawa sought help from the Texas and United States governments, but found none. The 146 remaining Tonkawa returned to Oklahoma in 1870 to live on less than 100 government-allotted acres.

The Tonkawa suffered and declined as a tribe during this period largely because Anglos were so successful at pioneering in the north-central Texas region. The Mexican government first began settling the area that later became Ellis County by issuing a land certificate in the fall of 1834 as a grant of payment for legal services rendered to Judge Thomas Jefferson Chambers, originally of Virginia. Within a month, the Mexican government gave out two other grants, one to Rafael de la Pena and the other to Alexander de la Garza, both Mexican citizens, and charged the men with colonizing the territory. Only Chambers visited and eventually settled on his grant; the other men sold their lands to speculators who, in turn, attempted to attract settlers.

William Welsh, a Methodist preacher and the first known white to take up permanent residence in the area, was squatting illegally along Waxahachie Creek

A group of local women gathered along one of the county's many creeks to gather pecans. Socializing proved difficult during the 1840s and 1850s because of the great distances between settlers' homes. When an opportunity to get together arose, few of the area's ladies stayed home.

Waxahachie's first citizen, Emory Rogers, immigrated to the Waxahachie Creek area in 1847 from Alabama. A leader from the town's inception, Rogers donated the land on which the city now stands and served in the Texas Rangers and the Confederate army.

near present-day Sardis with his wife and five children when William R. Howe arrived in 1843. Howe, the first Anglo to settle legally in the territory that later became Ellis County, applied for and received a conditional third-class head right of 640 acres in January 1840 from Harrisburg (now Harris) County Board of Land Commissioners. Like many newcomers, Howe applied under the Republic of Texas law that allowed citizens to receive free land who had arrived in the newly created nation prior to 1840. According to the 1836 Republic of Texas Constitution, all heads of families living in the region before March 2, 1836, the day Texas declared itself independent from Mexico, could receive a first-class head right of a league (4,428 acres) and a labor (177 acres). The Republic issued other head right certificates. For example, the new nation gave Howe 640 acres because he had immigrated after October 1837, but before January 1840. These land bounties formed the core of Texas's attempts to settle the Republic with Anglos.

Although Howe settled in the area first, another early pioneer, Emory W. Rogers, proved far more important to the future formation of Ellis County and the city of Waxahachie. Rogers received a third-class head right from the Board of Land Commissioners in Montgomery County, similar to Howe's head right, in December 1839. Rogers first saw his land, then surveyed it as a part of the Robertson District, in 1844. Two years later, he moved his family to Smith's Station (a Texas Rangers fort on Richland Creek near present-day Milford, southwest of Waxahachie), rented a farm, and raised a crop. The next year, he hired a laborer, Thomas Stevens, to prepare his head right for the spring's planting season. In the fall, Rogers moved his family to their homestead and they spent most of 1847 living in a tent while building a log cabin.

Emory Rogers, his wife Nancy, and their six children (the Rogers eventually had nine children) found that their 640 acres supplied most of their homesteading needs. Bordered by Waxahachie Creek (Rogers later purchased almost 400 additional acres north of the creek, selling 300 acres on the southern side), Rogers's land was cut by a naturally fed spring. With an ample and fresh water supply readily available, the family turned to growing crops on their land. By April, Rogers, like the other settlers staking claims along Waxahachie and Chambers Creeks, had plowed up several acres of prairie using a wooden plow and a yoke of six oxen. Using an axe, he formed a hole, dropped in his corn seed, and covered it by tamping the ground with his foot. The work was physically demanding and a single man by himself could only improve a dozen

Nancy Rogers, wife of Emory Rogers, was one of the first women to settle in the territory. Born in Alabama, Rogers immigrated to Texas with her husband after the nation declared itself independent from Mexico. She went on to have nine children, operate Waxahachie's first hotel, and found the first Methodist church in the city.

acres—those men who had sons old enough to work in the fields might clear and plant up to 50 acres.

By early June, when the corn stalks were just beginning to put on their first true leaves, the Rogers family found their prairie land alive with buffalo. Everywhere they turned, not 100 yards from their cabin's front door, buffalo gathered. The large animals had migrated each year from the west for hundreds of years to feed, mate, and rest along the waterways of Waxahachie Creek. The black bear joined the large beasts, prowling for newborn or sick buffalo, feasting before their winter's hibernation. The pioneers in the area harvested the buffalo—shooting them for their meat, skinning and baling the hides, hauling them the 100 or more miles to the Red River where the hides were traded for wheat, ammunition, and other staples.

The buffalo, so plentiful in the mid-1840s, had virtually disappeared by 1850. Anglos came quickly to the area and once settlement began, most of the wild animals in the region disappeared. Along with the buffalo, the settlers killed the bears, antelope, hogs, and turkey for their flesh and hides. Deer, especially plentiful when the first Americans immigrated to the territory, were hunted for their meat, which was eaten fresh or dried into jerky. The deer hides could be sold

Settlers during the early years often met along one of the county's many creeks to socialize, like this gathering at Waxahachie Creek c. *1890. This photograph was taken during one of the many picnics that occurred after the harvest was brought in when the farmers could relax for a short while.*

or traded for goods or fashioned into shirts and pants for men and moccasins for men, women, and children.

The settlers continued to change the natural environment throughout the decade. More Americans arrived looking for land, but others brought the implements necessary to begin small scale manufacturing and business enterprises. By the time Emory Rogers built his cabin in 1847, a gristmill had been established near the small community of Dallas (at the time, Dallas consisted of two small log cabins with a population of 12 souls), no more than 30 miles north of Rogers's cabin, that ground wheat by horse or ox power. The mill's presence meant that the pioneers could grow their own bread—up until this point, they either purchased wheat or relied solely on the corn that they grew and then ground at home for breadstuffs—although the process remained time consuming and labor intensive.

Wheat grew readily in the blackland soil, but despite the mill's presence, processing the grain was still difficult. Farmers began by cutting the crop with hand cradles, then they whipped it out with a flail or tramped it out with horses, accomplished by cleaning off a section of ground near the wheat stacks, laying down a bed of wheat in a circle. Then the younger boys would ride or lead horses around the circle, encouraging them to trample the crop while the men stirred the wheat with pitchforks. After the wheat was separated, the straw was raked off and the grain piled in the center. The process continued until the entire crop was thrashed. Then the men—the landowner and neighbors—cleaned the wheat by building a platform and letting the grain blow through the air a little at a time, landing on a sheet on the ground, so that the wind would blow the chaff away. Once free of the chaff, the wheat would be washed to remove any impurities and then dried so that it was ready to be hauled to the mill to be ground.

Generally, neighbors helped each other out with time consuming tasks like thrashing. They would begin on one farmer's fields and then work their way around to all the fields. While the men and their sons worked under the hot sun, their wives and daughters prepared a noonday meal that now appears staggering in our more fat and calorie conscious present. Wild game, chicken (often deep fried in lard), ham, or salt pork (and sometimes several different meats) with a pan gravy might be accompanied by potatoes and other vegetables from the kitchen garden, home canned goods, biscuits, and freshly baked fruit and buttermilk pies. Cold water, sometimes fresh milk for the children, and strong coffee encouraged the men to continue the work through the evening, usually taking a cold dinner of leftovers from the noon meal. Although their homes might be 3 to 5 miles apart, these neighbors helped each other to accomplish tasks, like thrashing wheat to ready it for the mill, that were too difficult for one family to undertake.

Although the mill was one of the first commercial enterprises begun in the area, others soon followed. Hans Smith, who had immigrated from Missouri, opened the first dry goods store in the area within a year. Smith purchased supplies in Houston and hauled them in a wagon drawn by oxen back to his cabin. Neighbors, who included settlers living within a 30-mile radius, could then purchase staples

William and Anna Hawkins, two of the area's original settlers, lived in one of the first homes in Waxahachie. The couple and their children traveled by wagon from Indiana through the Mississippi Valley to establish a settlement along Hawkin's Spring, just east of Midlothian. After being elected the county's first chief justice, Hawkins moved his family into this house in Waxahachie.

like coffee, sugar, tobacco, salt, soda, fabric for clothing, ammunition, and gunpowder locally, saving them a great deal of time and eliminating many of the risks involved with long distance travel, such as threats from wild animals, Native Americans, and roaming robbers.

All of the changes in the area guaranteed that more Americans would immigrate to the region. Since Emory Rogers's cabin was on an old Shawnee trail, the house quickly became a way station for travelers and a social gathering place for those who chose to homestead in the area. Warm and friendly, Emory and Nancy Rogers welcomed all who came their way. Many people stopped at the Rogers's home for a warm meal and a clean bed for the night. Others came to talk religion with Nancy, who organized the first Methodist church in the area in her home in 1849. She often held Bible classes and sometimes did a little preaching herself; itinerant pastors were few and far between. If not discussing theology with Nancy, travelers and neighbors talked politics or debated the latest Native American attacks with Emory.

Although homesteaders farther west were often harassed by Native Americans, particularly the Apache and Comanche, settlers along Waxahachie Creek never experienced any serious attacks because the men in the area had formed three companies that patrolled a line from Richland Creek to Chambers Creek, and then up to the timbers along the Trinity River. Twice a day for more than four years, men under the command of Texas Ranger Thomas Smith rode the line and protected the settlements. The only raid of any note occurred in 1847 and settlers laughingly referred to it in later years as "Mitchell's War." Around 30 Native Americans broke through the Ranger's line at an unguarded point and demanded tobacco and food from a man named Mitchell, who served as the local postmaster since his house was on the old Austin road. About that time, the mail carrier, a young lad of 16, rode up and having spotted the attackers confronting Mitchell, sped his horse from cabin to cabin spreading the word that Mitchell was being attacked. The Rangers were notified and gave chase, but lost the braves in the timbers along the Brazos River. Mitchell laughed along with the others about the scare the young boy had induced by exaggerating the attack, making the story more dramatic with each retelling.

Although the threat of Native American attacks frightened the settlers, prairie fires proved a far more dangerous enemy. The raging flames frequently swept across the country engulfing the tall prairie grass that measured between a man's knee and waist, covering the land from river to river. The extreme temperatures and drought conditions of late August and September proved a perfect breeding ground, combined with the southerly winds that prevailed in the fall, a single fire could leave a blackened world in its wake. One settler described a prairie fire in the fall of 1847, claiming, "the fire came in a breast a mile wide roaring like a tornado, curling, surging, and catching fifty yards away and then on again with the speed of the wind."

Much had changed along Waxahachie Creek in the six years since whites had begun to carve out settlements. A frontier outpost with virtually no Anglo habitation in 1844, the area had boomed. The population by the end of the decade had increased to nearly 100 families. The first generation of pioneers had tamed the prairies, successfully growing crops, making a living, and raising families. The land, once a wilderness teeming with animals and Native Americans, had come under their control. These men and women introduced their version of civilization to the frontier in the form of local governments, churches, and schools.

2. Blessed with the Most Civic-Minded People

Hans Smith stepped to the podium between loud cheering and whistling to deliver the oration at the county's first Fourth of July celebration. "This community has been blessed," Smith began, with the most "civic minded people . . ." but he could not continue, the crowd clapped so loudly that he was forced to wait. The citizens of the newly formed town of Waxahachie, seat of the recently created Ellis County, celebrated in grand fashion on July 4, 1851. Having been in existence for a year, the town's population had exploded, farming had expanded, and new businesses started daily. Most of the county's residents had turned out for the first annual Independence Day celebration. They listened to speakers—local men like Hans Smith, a businessman and the first representative to the state legislature from neighboring Navarro County—and joined together for a community barbecue and watched the children play. The next ten years proved equally exciting for the new town. Growth continued; the people of Waxahachie developed a local government, diversified their agriculture, created new business opportunities, and began building churches, schools, and social organizations.

In the fall of 1849, several men from the Waxahachie Creek settlement approached Edward H. Tarrant, a state representative, about forming a new county. Texans found traveling long distances difficult, time consuming, and often dangerous, and their state government in Austin often seemed as far away as did their national government in Washington, D.C. Local county governments held an importance far beyond what they do today, but even traveling to distant county seats proved prohibitive for many Texans. As populations increased, local citizens got together and discussed the possibilities of forming new and smaller counties. In 1836, the Waxahachie Creek area was surveyed in Milam County, but the next year, it was reapportioned as part of Robertson County. By 1846, it was included in Navarro County. Three years later, the area had grown to such a degree that many locals believed they could get the 100 necessary signatures to form a new county.

Edward Tarrant agreed to draw up the bill if the men could muster the signatures. Hans Smith and Benjamin Hawkins rode on horseback from cabin to cabin asking qualified voters to sign their petition to create a new county.

An early street scene of downtown Waxahachie, the photograph reflects the city's increased importance as a commercial and trading hub in the region.

So few people lived in the area, Hawkins rode a second time, canvassing each house again. He was successful on his last search and found 100 voters. With the necessary signatures in hand, Tarrant presented his bill to create a new county to a special session of the state legislature in December 1849. Just five days before Christmas, Texas lawmakers voted to create Ellis County, named in honor of Richard Ellis, president of the Constitutional Convention in 1836 when Texas declared its independence from Mexico. Peter H. Bell signed the bill into law just one day after he had been sworn in as governor.

The legislature appointed nine commissioners from the area, including Smith and Hawkins, to organize the county. The law demanded that a local government be established that was within 5 miles of the geographic center of the county and that the seat, no matter where it was located, be named Waxahachie, a derivation of the Tonkawa words *a-wash* (buffalo) and *cha-kow-titch* (creek) that had been translated through the Waco language and then Anglicized. The word honored the major waterway through the new region, the life-giving force for the early American settlers and the Native Americans and animals that had lived there before them, and formalized the Anglo spelling of the creek.

Ellis County citizens proposed three sites for the county seat: Grove Creek, Reagor Spring's Place, and the Rogers' cabin. All three met the geographic requirements, but only Emory Rogers volunteered to donate 60 acres from which to create the new town. On August 5, 1850, 96 voters came out to cast their ballots and they overwhelmingly chose the Rogers' site as the location of the county seat. A long-time stopover for travelers and a social gathering place for neighbors, the Rogers' cabin seemed a logical choice.

Less than 15 days later, the first county officials were sworn into office. William Hawkins, who had led a wagon train of settlers from Indiana in 1848 through the Mississippi Valley to pioneer Hawkins's springs just north of Midlothian (ten miles west of Waxahachie), was elected chief justice. Larkin Newton, Henry Trimble, and James L. Berry were made commissioners; Benjamin Hawkins, William's son and the man who had twice ridden through the county looking for signatures, was made county clerk; and William H.H. Bradford was elected sheriff.

As one of their first acts, the new commissioners hired Richard C. Donaldson to survey the 60 acres donated by Emory and Nancy Rogers into a public square, streets, and town lots. The men next proposed to build a road from Waxahachie to Taos in Navarro County and then discussed the building of the first courthouse. At this point, the new government officials were holding court in the Rogers' log cabin. To gain legitimacy, a separate governmental building was needed immediately, so the men hired Joseph Whittenberg to build a courthouse and have it fitted and ready for use by the first court session, scheduled for the third Monday in October.

The new county's first courthouse was built by Joseph Whittenberg in 1850. The log structure was hauled from Dallas County and reassembled for $59. The small building, 16 feet by 18 feet, stood across the street from Emory and Nancy Rogers' cabin and handled all the county's business for three years.

Knowing that he had less than two months and that wood for building was scarce locally, Whittenberg purchased a cedar log building that had been used as a church and school in Dallas County and hauled it intact to the new county square. After he made some alterations, the building met the commissioners' requirements: it was made of logs, was at least 16 by 18 feet in size, and cost no more than $59. By October 28, the first day of court in the new county, Whittenberg's courthouse was ready.

Early that morning, John Ranson left his farm for town. Like many of the local men, he was anxious to see his new government in action. His wife Sarah was surprised then when she heard footsteps on her front porch. "What did you forget?" she called out, expecting to hear the familiar Irish cadences of her husband's voice, still laced with the brogue despite the years he had spent in the States. "Ma'am," she heard instead, "I'm the census taker and I'm hear to talk with you about your home and family."

Sarah left the boiling water. Monday was wash day and, even with the help of one of the female slaves, laundry was always a difficult and time consuming task. "Yes, of course, come in. Can I get you something? A cup of coffee? A slice of bread?"

Sarah sat with the census taker most of the morning. She told him about her husband John, who had immigrated to the United States from Ireland when he was only 23. "He's been in the States for twenty-one years," she laughed, and "oh he does have the luck of the Irish!" Many Irish had come to the United States in the last 20 years, she explained, because they had suffered terribly between the potato famine and the English.

"Yes, John and I have been quite happy together," she said. "We met soon after he arrived—that was in South Carolina—and were married . . . He's a farmer, you know, and we struggled at first . . . Moved from South Carolina to North Carolina, then on to Tennessee. My first boy, Robert, still lives in Tennessee. Then we came on here to Texas in 1849.

"Now that was a trip I don't ever want to make again!" Sarah laughed, but the census taker could see a sad distant look in her eyes. "My youngest boy, William, died on the way," she said. "We all came down sick . . . After William, my middle son's wife died and so did one of our slaves . . . We thought we'd never make it here, but the people have been so kind—so understanding . . . They embraced us as soon as we arrived and shared our grief.

"That was about the same time talk started up about creating this new county you're now recording," she explained, "and such change has taken place in just one year! Why my son John Jr., he's twenty-four now and helps his Daddy here on the farm, talks on and on about the potential of this great county . . . Last year we could hardly muster one hundred signatures on the petition and now look at us!"

The census taker knew what Sarah meant. By the time he had made his rounds to every family, he found that Ellis County had grown to include 989 residents—912 white and free black individuals and 77 slaves. John Ranson was

One of Waxahachie's earliest grocery stores, Bohanans offered customers an assortment of dry goods, including molasses, sugar, tea, and coffee. Women often traded their chicken eggs and butter they had churned for credit to purchase ready-made cloth and other sewing notions.

not the only foreign immigrant. Three other Irish had settled in the county, as well as a man from England and a woman from Honduras. The other residents were from the United States, but they represented virtually all the organized districts in 1850—immigrants hailed from 22 different states, although most came from Tennessee or Missouri. Almost all of these individuals were farmers who grew primarily wheat, corn, oats, and sweet potatoes. Many had begun to raise stock cattle and most had hogs for home consumption.

Although Ellis County's economy was based on agriculture, Waxahachie had developed a prosperous commercial district. A.D. Marchbanks arrived in the city in 1851 and immediately erected a shanty that became the town's first dry goods store. He brought up a stock of miscellaneous goods from Galveston—barrels of molasses, sugar, calico cloth, and ammunition—and opened his door for business. By the end of the year, the town boasted, in addition to Marchbank's store, three blacksmiths, two mechanics, another merchant, three stock raisers, a doctor, five carpenters, two attorneys, one bricklayer, one minister, and one tailor.

Waxahachie continued to grow and optimism remained high, despite the swarm of locusts that descended on the county in 1853. Farmers later reported that they heard a low buzzing sound way off in the distance, a sound like the wailing of a high wind. Puzzled, most watched curiously as a dark reddish cloud slowly emerged from the northwest and traveled toward them at a rapid rate. At first, grasshoppers dropped singly from the sky, but before long, they fell to the ground like a heavy rain, 2 to 3 inches thick. More filled the sky, casting a shadow across the land. The grasshoppers began to eat the vegetation and, within three days, with the earth so brown and bare it looked like it had been scorched by fire, the insects began to tackle everything else that might be edible. Like a machine, they devoured laundry hanging on the line, curtains in screenless windows, and even tried to eat wooden hoe handles. All work stopped—as much from the inconvenience as from the odor. The grasshoppers smelled strongly and the smell invaded the flesh of the animals that ate them. The hogs, chickens, ducks, and wild birds took on the odor, and their flesh proved inedible for months.

Although the locusts of 1853 laid eggs that hatched the following spring, the county did not suffer as greatly. Other swarms of grasshoppers descended on the prairies in latter years, but never again in such numbers.

Having weathered their first major calamity, the citizens of Waxahachie renewed their building energies. The county had grown so much by 1853 that the court commissioned the building of a new courthouse. The community replaced the original log cabin courthouse with a new frame two-story structure designed with a dogtrot. Offices were established downstairs and court was held upstairs.

The growing city built a new courthouse within a few years. The larger structure reflected the increased prominence of Waxahachie.

When court was not in session, the town's children played on the lawn and ran up and down the stairs, waiting their turn to sit on the judge's bench. While the judge might not have enjoyed finding bits of the children's candy left behind in his courtroom, he was increasingly less bothered by them.

By the mid-1850s, the first rural schools were established in the county. Children purchased their own textbooks; the *Blue Black Speller* being one of the most commonly used texts, and wrote with cedar pencils on slate boards. These one-room schools were simple affairs, sessions timed to the seasons' rhythms of planting and harvesting. Teachers spent most of their days with recitations, grouping the children, who might vary widely in age, according to their abilities. The students sang religious and popular songs, memorized poetry and short prayers, and competed weekly against each other in spelling bees. Parents were often divided about sending their children to school. Many needed to keep their families at home, their labor necessary to successfully farm their prairie land.

Pioneers established rural schools in Ellis County as early as the 1850s. These children enjoyed recess after their lunch break by playing games like "whip the snake" and "ring around the rosy." Most of their school day was spent inside the one-room building working through the Blue Black Speller *and writing sums on slate boards with cedar pencils.*

Even before Nancy Rogers established the first congregation, pioneers along Waxahachie Creek gathered to worship together. This early baptism scene shows a group of believers practicing "old style religion."

Others, those who believed that an education was essential for their children's futures, sent their boys and girls, hoping that they would learn to read, write, and do enough arithmetic to gain a measure of confidence and skill.

But even before the first schools were created, the people of Waxahachie formed churches. In the mid-1840s, during the summer, settlers living within a 60-mile radius gathered along Red Oak Creek near the settlement of Ovilla (about 10 miles northwest of Waxahachie) for religious camp meetings—what they described as "old style religion." Itinerant preachers held services in the evenings under a grouping of shade trees or a makeshift arbor of grapevines, and peoples of all Christian denominations worshipped together. These meetings sometimes lasted a week with preaching in the evening and Bible study throughout the day. The pioneers set up tents and brought provisions to last them during their stay, while enjoying the sense of worship and community fellowship.

The first church organized in the county now stands on the site of the most popular camp meeting location. Ovilla citizens organized Shiloh Cumberland Presbyterian Church in 1846 and built a small permanent structure for their meetings. Although the church was too far removed from Waxahachie Creek for its settlers to attend regularly, they did continue to go to the summer camp meetings held each year at the church.

Nancy Rogers organized the Methodist Episcopal Church in 1849, the first place of fellowship for the settlers living along Waxahachie Creek. Early members included Mrs. Rogers, Milley Weaver, Jonathan and Ventura Prince, David Fearis,

Prior to the railroads coming to Ellis County in 1879, most agricultural production in the county focused on grains, including wheat, rye, and maize. This early thrashing scene shows the community's commitment to coming together to bring in the summer's wheat harvest.

Norman Whittenberg, Charles Barker, Rebecca Barker, and Margaret Barker. Nancy often led the Bible study herself, and she welcomed all ministers who passed by to stop, stay in her home, and preach to the local people. Within two years, the small congregation was worshipping in a separate structure on a lot donated by Emory and Nancy Rogers.

As the town grew, so did its need to represent different denominations. A Cumberland Presbyterian Church organized in the city in 1853, a Baptist Church began meeting in 1861, and an Episcopal Church formed in 1876. During these early years, all of the congregations met in the Methodist Church, each taking their turn and enjoying the building one Sunday a month, sharing in its maintenance and upkeep.

Nancy and Emory Rogers had prospered since they first looked at their head right in 1847. Both born in Alabama, the young couple (the census taker reported that Emory was 37 years old and Nancy 29 in 1850) had always shared their home, meals, and hearts with passers-by. They made the arrangement formal in 1855 when they constructed the first hotel in Waxahachie at the site of their original cabin on the corner of Main and College Streets. The Rogers House, as they called their establishment, first advertised in the *Dallas Herald* in June 1856 and promised clean beds, good food, and that visitors could "talk politics with Emory to your heart's content." The two-story frame structure was built of planed logs brought from the Trinity River bottom and East Texas, and serviced travelers and district court personnel. Emory Rogers continued to farm his land; he had more than 200 acres under cultivation (mostly wheat and rye) and owned 30 horses. His son Tandy helped Nancy in the hotel most days, although their slaves performed the hardest labor.

Throughout the 1850s, as the general population increased, so did the number of slaves in the county. Very few of Waxahachie's citizens owned any slaves in the early part of the decade and those that did had only one or two. A few prosperous families, like Emory and Nancy Rogers, might have owned between three and ten slaves, but because most of the town's residents had immigrated from upper southern states, like Tennessee and Missouri where there was little large-scale plantation agriculture in place and, therefore, no need for large numbers of slaves, they had no background in plantation culture. Few of Waxahachie's residents cultivated enough land or were wealthy enough to warrant holding large numbers of slaves.

The community's demographics changed, however, toward the latter part of the decade. More and more, Deep South southerners moved to Waxahachie and these individuals began purchasing plantation-sized landholdings. They started experimenting on a small scale with growing cotton and they brought in large numbers of slaves. The changed nature of the population by 1860 reflected a move toward plantation agriculture, visibly reflected by the more than 700 slaves living and working in the county by the end of the decade.

This photograph shows cotton wagons, c. 1882. Local farmers began for the first time to commit significant amounts of acreage to the planting of cotton after the Civil War. The steadily increasing commodity prices associated with the fiber made the crop profitable to grow in the region.

For example, Thomas C. Neel brought the first large number of slaves into the county in 1855. A small but compactly built man with piercing dark eyes, Neel had been born and raised in Georgia, where he taught school and farmed until 1854. When hearing of the fertile soil and healthy climate in Texas, he brought his family and slaves to Harrison County. After touring the blackland prairie, he purchased several hundred acres outside of Waxahachie. Within a few years, he had created a large plantation, fencing most of the acreage and bringing the land under cultivation. He began growing cotton almost immediately, though he derived most of his income from wheat. Owning 80 slaves and one of the largest plantations in the county, Neel enjoyed a prestige, both social and political, that few others in Waxahachie shared.

By the eve of the Civil War, men like Thomas Neel, though a relative newcomer to the city, held positions of power and influence at the local level, power that was used to sway voters to secede from the Union. Waxahachie had boomed during the 1850s—from its inception as the new county seat to its position as the commercial and trading hub of the region. The town was poised to continue its dramatic growth, but political and ideological issues on the national level stalled further expansion. Swept up by the fury of a civil war and its aftermath, the people of Waxahachie were blown along with the winds of destiny.

Waxahachie sits on a belt of extremely fertile soil known as the Blackland Prairie. Although settlers knew how valuable the land was, it was not until the invention of the metal plow that farmers could till the thick clay soil to plant crops.

3. Let Us Strike for Freedom

Anna Hawkins pushed the coals around in the trap door underneath the oven and laid another piece of wood on the ashes. She then reached her arm, almost to the elbow, into the belly of the stove to test the heat. She had peeled peaches all morning, slicing them into quarter moons, and mixed them with a little sugar and cinnamon. When the fruit was ready, she blended flour and salt with some of the sweet butter she had churned the day before, making a pastry to cover the peaches. The stove's temperature had to be just right—not so hot that the crust would burn before the peaches softened and caramelized, but not so cool that the pastry would not cook through. Anna thought back to her young married days when her inexperience meant many a burned biscuit, but now at 61, having raised 11 children—9 of them hungry boys—she knew exactly how the heat should feel on her arm to bake a perfect cobbler.

It was the boys that Anna was worried about feeding that hot August day. Not just her own two, John and George, but all the boys from the county who had enlisted with W.H. Parsons to form a cavalry regiment. The men were encamped along Rockett's Spring (about ten miles north of Waxahachie) waiting to choose their officers and receive instructions from the state. Anna and dozens of other ladies from around the county baked for the boys and brought them what comforts they could manage. In August 1861 no one, not even Anna who had known a great many of life's cruel lessons, imagined the horror that the war would bring to the country.

Anna and her husband William Hawkins had been one of the first families to settle in the area. They had prospered and lived contentedly, as did most of the people who came to Ellis County, but found their lives and community turned upside-down with the coming of the Civil War. Slave insurrections and uprisings threatened the social order in the north-central Texas area in 1860, followed quickly by a renewal of Native American attacks. Waxahachie's citizens, frightened by the rapid changes, sought desperately to find some source of stability. By the time Lincoln took office in 1861, the people of Ellis County had committed their lives and fortunes to the Confederacy. The county eventually sent four companies of men to fight in the war. Back home, Texans endured a great many deprivations, but they did not suffer the physical damage

The coming of the railroad proved the single most significant economic factor to occur in Waxahachie. Two engineers pause while oiling their locomotive to pose for a photograph. Notice that the drive wheels are taller than the men, a necessity to achieve the high speeds on a crack passenger run.

so devastating to states like Virginia, South Carolina, and Georgia. The state recovered relatively quickly after the war and no city more so than Waxahachie. The war years proved to be only a pause in the county's continued growth and expansion.

In many ways, Waxahachie actually became more southern after the war than she had been before. Large numbers of immigrants flooded into the town and county in the post-war years, many from the ravaged Deep South states, and they brought with them the heritage of growing cotton and the culture that accompanied it. For the first time, planters began cultivating large tracts of the fluffy white fiber, especially after Waxahachie's businessmen funded a Tap Rail Road that linked the town with the Houston and Texas Central. The county's farmers and commercial investors never looked back—they committed themselves and their land to King Cotton.

In 1860, almost 60 percent of the people living in Ellis County were from the upland south, and most of them owned small farms and no slaves. They found the soil good and fertile, and they grew so much grain that the county was the fourth largest wheat producer in the state. A minority of the county's population,

40 percent, hailed from the Deep South, and they brought cotton culture and a commitment to slave labor to the blackland prairies. There were 1,104 slaves in the county, but they were owned by only 197 individuals out of a total white population of 4,136. Of those who owned slaves, more than 75 percent had less than 5 slaves and only 26 people in the county held more than 10 slaves. Although a minority, these planters controlled most of the wealth in the county (measured most often in terms of slaves and real property), and they held a social and political position in the community that far outweighed their numbers.

When the "Texas Troubles" broke in July 1860, the town's upper class led the way in squelching the feared uprising and in seeking revenge. Over the course of two months, the most influential men in Waxahachie joined with similarly stationed men throughout the state, denouncing northern abolitionists' attempts to incite a slave rebellion in the state and bring down the planter class.

G.F. Marchbanks thumped the thermometer he had hung out on the porch in front of his hardware store. The temperature read well over 100 degrees and this was in the shade. It was just after 2:00 in the afternoon and most of the townsfolk had finished their Sunday noon meals and were relaxing out of the direct heat. The downtown square was deserted and Marchbanks had only come to his store out of restlessness. His wife Henrietta had drawn all the blinds in the house to block out as much of the sun as possible and then had taken herself off to rest. With little else to do and worried that he had not entered his last order into his

The Houston and Texas Central's hook-up with Waxahachie's Tap Railroad in 1879 proved pivotal in the county's move toward cotton growing.

books, Marchbanks walked to the store, trying to stay in the shade of the town's young trees.

Engrossed in his accounts, Marchbanks did not hear the shouts outside his store for several minutes. Finally noticing the commotion, he was shocked when he walked out and found the dusty streets around the square filled with men, many carrying buckets. A fire had been discovered at a dry goods store just a few doors down from Marchbanks Hardware and was quickly being put out. Word of the fire spread and the community rejoiced that night because the potentially devastating flames had been found and extinguished before any significant damage had occurred.

Marchbanks was surprised when later in the week he found a group of men waiting for him in front of his store. The men were discussing an account in the *Dallas Herald* that described a half dozen fires that had started in different Texas towns on the same day, July 8, at approximately the same time, 2:00 in the afternoon. Most of downtown Dallas had been destroyed in the worst fire; another had razed half of Denton's commercial square. The paper also reported fires at Pilot Point, Black Jack Grove, Ladonia, Milford, Austin, and in Fannin County. The *Herald's* editor, Charles R. Pryor, claimed that the fires were part of a larger abolitionist conspiracy to "devastate with fire and assassination, the whole of North Texas."

Acting on Pryor's advice, Texans across the state formed vigilante groups and began combing the slave quarters on the state's plantations. At the end of the week, a vigilante group in the eastern portion of the state caught several slaves burning a house and arrested them. The slaves quickly confessed to starting the fire and then detailed a plot organized by northern abolitionists to use fire and assassination to illicit a general slave rebellion in the state, which was to commence on election day in August.

The arrested slaves continued their tale of intrigue. Abolitionist preachers had circulated through Texas in 1859, they claimed, dividing the state into districts and appointing a white man who opposed slavery as special superintendent of each section. The superintendent controlled the slaves in his district and was responsible for organizing and preparing them to light the fires, assassinate their masters and their master's families, and then rise in a general rebellion.

By Friday, July 20, the people of Waxahachie were in a state of high excitement. The town nearly buzzed with the tension and all talk was of the conspiracy, particularly of the community's own fire and the culprits who might have started it. Local slaves, after having been interrogated, claimed that abolitionists had forced them to keep strychnine in their cabins so that they could poison the town's water supply—a secondary plot that had been planned for July 22 and included poisoning all the white people in Waxahachie. The slaves named their ringleader: an African-American man that the town's vigilante posse had found hiding out along Red Oak Creek. The vigilantes, with the support of the local law enforcement, rounded up the three slaves they believed most responsible for the insurrection in Waxahachie and prepared for a hanging.

The tall native grasses combined with the drought and extreme summer temperatures made prairie fires a dangerous threat to the new settlers. A small fire might blow up into a raging wall of flames a mile wide that would consume every house and tree in its path.

Tuesday, July 24 dawned brilliantly as locals gathered in front of the town's jail to watch their "vigilance committee," formed (as a Louisiana newspaper reported) of the "most respectable and responsible men of this county," mete out justice. They watched as three African-American men, Patrick, who had unrepentedly declared that he had started the fire on July 8; Sam Smith, an old preacher who had taken his master's last name; and Cato, a mean slave who had always been a troublemaker (so his master claimed), were led to the gallows. The newspapers later reported that all three men died calmly and without remorse. Patrick, giving one last spit of tobacco, boldly declared moments before the rope tightened around his neck that the fire "was just the beginning of the good work."

Patrick, Sam, and Cato were the first slaves hanged in Waxahachie over the Texas Troubles, but they were not the last. The *Houston Telegraph* reported that by the middle of August, 20 other slaves and 2 white men, one of whom worked at a local store and had given the slaves the strychnine to place in local wells, had been hanged also. The *Austin State Gazette* ran a letter by a Waxahachie gentleman who said that his town's vigilance committee had arrested more than 100 blacks and whites, questioned them, and punished them to varying degrees. The committee had discovered that northerners who were opposed to slavery had coerced the slaves, who were working for the Abolitionist Aid Society, with promises that after the whites had been killed, their land would be divided and distributed among the freed slaves.

Texans were shocked by the plot and talked endlessly about it throughout the remainder of the summer. One of the state's Congressmen, John H. Reagan, who lived in Palestine and would soon be chosen Confederate Postmaster General, wrote to his brother about the abolitionist's plan. He said the slaves were told to:

> kill as many people as they could on Sunday night before the election, and then on the day of the election [August 6] to burn the houses and to kill as many of the women and children as they could while the men were gone to the election, and then kill the men as they returned.

At the time, southerners considered the uprising to be the most serious slave insurrection threat since Nat Turner had rebelled in 1831 and killed 55 whites, beginning with his own master and his master's family. In all, more than a dozen Texas towns experienced some type of fire or vandalism that was attributed to the abolitionist plot to end slavery. Over 30 verifiable hangings (those where first-hand witness reports are reliable) occurred in northern Texas between July 8 and August 31, though second-hand reports suggest that the actual number may have exceeded more than 100.

Northern anti-slavery advocates denied the charges, continually claiming that the fires were an unfortunate accident and that abolitionists had not planned

The Knights of the Golden Circle formed a chapter in Waxahachie prior to the Civil War. Some of the area's leading citizens joined the organization, the same men who were introducing the growing of cotton into the region. The KGC often discussed politics and the institution of slavery at local cotton gins like this one on the outskirts of Ovilla, north of Waxahachie.

any general revolt. They argued that "prairie matches started the fires," a newly introduced phosphorus match that was highly unstable and volatile. The matches, northern abolitionists claimed, had spontaneously ignited because of the unusually high temperatures. Reports indicate that it had been 110 degrees in Dallas at the time of the fire on July 8.

The northern claims had some validity. The prairie matches, as they were called, had been known to spontaneously combust. For example, matches had ignited in William Oldham's store, located not far from Marchbanks Hardware in Waxahachie on the square, one afternoon right in front of two clerks and "Old Billy" Oldham. The clerks took the matches outside and laid them on the sidewalk—there, directly in the summer sun's heat, most ignited within a matter of minutes and a few burst into flames as soon as they touched the hot pavement.

Texans ignored northern claims and the local evidence. The political climate at the time dictated that any suggestion of a slave uprising would be taken seriously and dealt with summarily. John Brown's raid on Harper's Ferry, Virginia (now West Virginia) had occurred only nine months before and distrust of northerners had never been so high or widespread throughout the south. Once the suggestion had been made that the fires were linked to an abolitionist plot, no evidence was needed (and no hard evidence was ever gathered) to arrest, question, punish, and even execute suspected blacks and whites.

The Texas Troubles invoked a rising fear among all southerners that no northerner could be trusted because they might be abolitionists. In response to the panic in the aftermath of the slave revolt in Texas, membership grew in a secret organization known as the Knights of the Golden Circle (KGC), which had grown slowly since 1854 when it was created, and swelled in 1859. The brainchild of Virginia–born doctor and newspaper editor George W.L. Bickley, the KGC proposed to establish a slave empire throughout the United States, West Indies, Mexico, and parts of Central America. The ring (or circle) of land encompassed more than 2,400 miles and would have given its leaders a monopoly on the world's supply of cotton, sugar, rice, coffee, and tobacco.

Most of Waxahachie's male upper-class citizens joined together and formed a local chapter (or "castle" as they were secretly known) of the KGC. In all, 32 chapters were formed in Texas in 27 different counties, but mainly in the state's largest cities such as Dallas, Austin, Houston, Marshall, and San Antonio. Locally, the KGC continued to feed on Texans' fears of a large slave rebellion, particularly by holding meetings and torchlight parades after dark. As a national organization, the KGCs proposed to launch an invasion against Mexico and began arming at the chapter level, but the invasion never occurred.

Many of Waxahachie's political and business leaders joined the Knights in the aftermath of the Texas Troubles as a means of stabilizing their community. These men found even more reason to distrust the Union government, however, when a series of Native American attacks, more vicious than Ellis Countians had ever known, occurred in Parker and Jack Counties (west and northwest of Fort Worth) less than 70 miles from the Waxahachie Creek area. The two counties requested aid from the state government and the governor requested that Emory Rogers commission a company of men under the auspices of the Texas Rangers. Rogers led 24 volunteers from Ellis County and rode off toward Belknap on the frontier. After arriving, the attachment from Ellis County found the conditions to be far worse than newspapers had reported, and Rogers wrote home requesting that more men be organized and that they should bring more supplies. He blamed the federal government, claiming that it was too busy with other issues to aid its citizens against Native American deprivations. In response to his letter, Waxahachie organized another volunteer company of men who canvassed the city for food and provisions, then joined Rogers's men in Jacksboro, the county seat of Jack County.

These incidents, the supposed slave uprising and abolitionist plot, the sudden interest in the Knights of the Golden Circle's plan to create a slave empire, and the Native American attacks taken separately might have aroused Texans' emotions, but individually they would not have climaxed into something as drastic as secession. The combined force of the Native American assaults and the threat of a northern–led slave revolt caused the state's citizens, including the people of Waxahachie, to suffer a crisis in confidence with the United States government. Further, it helps to explain in part why a state that voted in 1859 for Sam Houston as governor, a man who was a staunch Unionist, could choose just one year later to secede from the United States, join the Confederacy, and offer itself up to a civil war.

The men of Waxahachie walked to the voting polls solemnly on November 6, 1860. An itinerant preacher visiting the town recorded the moment in his diary writing: "the men were calm, fully aware that this might be the last presidential election that they would vote in as a united country." Most Texans chose John C. Breckinridge as their presidential candidate, a Kentucky politician who was serving as vice president. Their votes had little impact because the ticket was split four ways and no nominee had garnered a national following. By midnight, Abraham Lincoln's victory was clear. In the final count, he had only 39 percent of the popular vote, but a clear majority with 180 electoral votes in the Electoral College. The uncommon common man had become president and, although he was a moderate on the slave issue and clearly against abolitionism, Lincoln's election foreshadowed future policy.

Soon after the presidential election, a special convention was held in Charleston, South Carolina, where the delegates voted an Ordinance of Secession, declaring the state's alliance with the United States dissolved. By February 1861, six more states had declared that they were seceding from the Union. Texas was the last of the seven to act because its governor, Sam Houston, had refused to assemble a special convention. Secessionist leaders in the state called an irregular session, circumventing Houston, and authorized a referendum on disunion.

Waxahachie sent two delegates to the special convention, which was held on January 28, 1861: Thomas C. Neel, one of the wealthiest planters and slave owners in the county, and Amzi Bradshaw, who had practiced law in the town since the mid-1850s. Both men, representing the desire of the community, spoke in favor of secession. The next month, Texans voted overwhelmingly to secede. In Waxahachie, 527 people voted in favor of secession and 172 opposed. The ballots represented only 66 percent of the men eligible to vote in the referendum, but of those that had cast their tickets, more than 75 percent had done so in favor of disunion. The county, with only slightly more than 1,000 slaves owned by only 21 percent of the population, had voted in opposition to what they considered to be the continued threats against the growth and expansion of the institution of slavery. What happened, it seemed, was that a determined minority in the state had taken advantage of an emotionally charged climate (following in the wake of Native American attacks and the threatened slave rebellion), acted quickly, and carried its program against an indecisive opposition. In Waxahachie, that emotionally charged minority represented the wealthiest and most elite citizens, most of whom had joined the Knights of the Golden Circle and held public meetings to arouse the sentiments of the yeoman farmers in the county.

Texas officially seceded on March 2, 1861, but a great many of its citizens had already begun to prepare themselves for battle. The women had been sewing uniforms and flags for weeks, and one Waxahachie woman recorded in her diary that her friend had been sewing cockades for the young soldiers' hats. Although she claimed not to know anything about politics, she believed that "it seems

This recruiting photograph shows recent volunteers from the Ellis County area for the Confederate army. In all, five units were formed from men from the county and the soldiers fought in more than 50 battles in the Trans-Mississippi Department.

The photograph (c. 1870) documents the west side of the downtown business district after the Civil War. Although growth had halted temporarily, merchants began to flood into the city during Reconstruction.

absolutely necessary that action must be taken in the case, and some measures taken to preserve the rights of the South."

Other Ellis Countians felt the same way. Jake Hesser, born and raised in Illinois, reported that his family had written, begging him to come back home, but he remained in Texas saying, "if war comes, I'll be for the rights of the South."

Jake Hesser remained true to his word and was one of more than 1,000 men who gathered at Rockett's Spring (about 10 miles north of Waxahachie) in August 1861. William Henry Parsons had been commissioned by the governor of Texas to form a cavalry regiment in the north-central part of the state, and men from the surrounding areas had joined with local volunteers, camping along the springs, waiting for officer elections. On September 11, 1861—election day—men, women, and children from throughout the county gathered to watch the proceedings. At 10:00 in the morning, a bugle sounded, and about 1,200 men marched, forming a hollow square. The soldiers elected their own officers, exercising their democratic liberties, and unanimously chose Parsons as their colonel. The men comprised ten companies, and three represented Ellis County exclusively: E—the Ellis County Grays; F—the Ellis and Johnson County Rangers; and H—the Ellis County Blues. Volunteers mustered in for one year's service, and they called themselves Parsons Brigade or the 12th Texas Cavalry Regiment.

The county treasury immediately provided $1,000 to outfit Companies E, F, and H with clothing, blankets, camp equipment, and horse shodding, and also provided an additional $300 for ammunition. Such funds helped to equip the men, but the money proved insufficient to meet the needs. Private individuals like Thomas Neel aided the cause as they could, giving funds, equipment, and horses to the soldiers, and using their plantation's resources to feed the men and the families they left behind.

As the war progressed, monetary and supply needs outstripped the county's citizens' ability to provide, but the shortages did not deter them from their cause. When nearby Dallas County initiated a new brigade, more Ellis County men volunteered. Forming Companies A and C of the 19th Texas Regiment, Waxahachie's boys made up in courage what they lacked in provisions.

Most of the soldiers Waxahachie sent to fight in the Civil War served in the Trans-Mississippi Department. They fought in almost 50 battles, many too small to have names. In Arkansas, Louisiana, and Mississippi, the men of Ellis County earned the reputation as one of the finest mounted units serving in the department. Acting mostly as scouts and outposts, the soldiers remained courageous in the face of overwhelming odds.

Life on the homefront in Waxahachie was far removed from the horrific fighting and death that the soldiers faced. Free from battles, the townspeople suffered greatest from shortages of food and materials, particularly cloth for clothing and other sewing supplies. Using what they had available, many a woman refashioned her dresses year after year, hoping to conceal the wear and tear. Others pulled out spinning wheels that had not been used in years and spun their own cotton and wove their own fabric.

Not only did the women in Waxahachie have to clothe themselves and their families, but also they were responsible for preparing clothing for their men who were fighting in the war. All the uniforms worn by the 12th Cavalry and the 19th Regiment were made by home production—mothers, wives, sisters, and sometimes slave women made shirts, pants, coats, blankets, and even tents. By mid-1862, it was virtually impossible to purchase any of these supplies ready-made, but the women of Waxahachie responded by making their own.

Henry Orr, a volunteer in the 12th, wrote to his family in Ellis County requesting that they make him and his brother "one coat each, one pair pants, two cotton shirts, one drawers for himself and one for his brother." He hoped that his mother could make the pants gray jeans or black with white sheep's wool, but wanted whatever color fabric she could manage. Little did Orr know that fabric was so scarce in Waxahachie that some men were wearing shirts made from tablecloths.

The women in Waxahachie could do little more than sew and pray for their fathers, husbands, and brothers, while their children, growing up in the town during the war, were at times oblivious to the significant national events. One of these children later recalled the war period by describing the excitement that she and her friends felt as they watched and listened for the stage horn as it rounded the hill and approached Waxahachie. During the war, a stagecoach passed through the town carrying mail and passengers en route from the Red River in the north to Austin in central Texas. Emory Rogers kept the relay station, and the coach always stopped to change horses and drop off mail. The young children took turns pretending to be the stagecoach driver, perched atop the carriage and directing the four spirited horses and passengers off on an exciting adventure.

The girl, Laura Parks Spaulding, dreamed of a real ride in a stagecoach and recounted her first trip, which came during the war. Headed for Waco (about 60 miles south of Waxahachie), the coach pulled out late in the afternoon and then stopped for the night at Chambers Creek. Leaving before sunrise, the driver stopped for breakfast in Hillsboro, rested and had lunch at a station kept by an "old Englishman and his wife" near the Brazos bottoms, changed horses, and arrived in Waco in the afternoon. Spaulding got her chance to ride the stagecoach because her uncle Felix had been placed in charge of all saddle and harness work for the Confederacy in Waco, a centrally-located town on the Brazos River. Another uncle had been detailed to work in the saddle shop, and he allowed Spaulding and her sister to travel with him to Waco. Milton Parks had to leave Ellis County to find war related work, a reflection of Waxahachie's lack of direct contact with the war. Except for the explosion of a powder mill that had been established in the town in cooperation with the Confederate State government, the town never experienced any war action.

The Confederacy's contract with the mill owner enabled him to make gunpowder on the halves with the southern government, but required him to supply all sulphur and saltpeter. The owner, William Rowen, who had immigrated to Texas from Ohio, built the mill in 1862 on Rogers Street (not far from where the First Baptist Church now stands) near a small branch of the Waxahachie Creek and next to the stagecoach stand. Using supplies requisitioned from an old horse mill and a blacksmith shop, the mill was powered by ten mules that worked on a treadmill, crushing and grinding the sulphur and saltpeter into hard cakes of powder.

In April 1863, less than a year after it began operating, the mill exploded suddenly and without warning. The townspeople, hearing the loud explosion, came running and found debris scattered for hundreds of yards. William Rowen had been killed instantly. A worker, J.G. Phillips, had been standing in the mill's doorway, and he died shortly afterward. Looking around for the third employee, the people found Dave Nance at the bottom of a nearby well. Nance, standing some distance from the mill, had been swept up in the fireball, but had kept presence of mind enough to jump into the well in an attempt to extinguish the fire ravaging his body. Although severely burned, Nance survived the incident.

Attempting to discover the cause of the explosion, local authorities came to believe that the mill had been deliberately sabotaged. Nance reported seeing a man in the area just before the explosion occurred. The mystery man quickly became the sheriff's chief suspect. Townspeople claimed he was a northerner who had been staying with his wife at the Rogers's hotel. The man had disappeared directly

Youngblood's Cash Grocery was one of many grocery stores to open shop in Waxahachie following the Civil War. Unlike most others, Youngblood's accepted only cash, no credit, on its sales and boasted that it was a true friend of the tenant or sharecropping farmer.

after the explosion and was never seen again. At the time, rumors circulated that he was a spy sent to destroy the powder mill. Today, a granite memorial marks the site of the powder mill on Rogers Street.

The stranger's presence in town was really not that unusual, though, because Waxahachie had a large migratory population during the war. As the fighting increased throughout Mississippi and Louisiana, thousands of refugees fled the destruction of the advancing Union soldiers. Many ran to Texas, and some passed through Ellis County, while others settled down and took up residence in Waxahachie. Even before these refugees bolted (most were women and children), many families had sent their slaves on ahead with overseers, fearing that their human property would be captured and put to work for the Union Army or that the slaves would run to the Union lines in search of freedom. The large number of refugees in the county swelled the population, and many decided to stay in Waxahachie after the war, purchasing land, which could still be had at relatively cheap prices, or taking up tenant or share-crop farming.

The Confederacy's dreams of victory and nationhood died on the battlefield. The years of Reconstruction, marked between 1865 and 1877, proved disheartening and difficult for many southerners, but not especially so for the people of Texas. With their land intact and unscathed by the war, towns like Waxahachie recovered quickly and began to grow and expand once again.

The people of Texas immediately tapped one of the state's greatest assets—its countless longhorn cattle. There had been no market for several years as Missouri and Kansas had closed their borders to Texas cattle in the 1850s because of the deadly Texas fever the cows carried. While Texas cattle appeared healthy in all respects, any midwestern cattle that were allowed to mingle with or near the longhorns fell ill with a fatal but unknown illness known as the Texas fever or the Texas cattle fever. The quarantine had greatly increased the number of cattle in Texas and, by 1867, when eastern demands for beef had grown to unprecedented heights, Texas cowmen were seeking new ways of getting their cattle to market.

Cattle had been one of the most profitable industries in Ellis County prior to the Civil War, so when word was spread that the Kansas Pacific Railroad had encouraged the building of pens and loading facilities near the tiny village of Abilene, Kansas—at the edge of the quarantine area—ranchers throughout the county responded and joined men and boys from across the state who drove their longhorns north along the Chisholm Trail, a loosely defined route, except at river crossings, from the Rio Grande to central Kansas. The path was named in honor of Scot-Cherokee Jesse Chisholm, who began using the trail as early as 1864 to haul trade goods to Native American camps south from his post near Witchita.

The Danielle family posed in front of their home in rural Ellis County shortly after the Civil War. The photograph reflects the family's rising economic situation and the general prosperity of the north Texas region during Reconstruction.

The Chisolm Trail never consisted of one single clearly marked path, but rather represented several old Native American trails. Once described as being tree-like, feeder trails from south Texas formed the roots, the main artery from San Antonio through Indian Territory (later renamed Oklahoma after achieving statehood) made up the trunk, and the branches were formed by the various railheads in Kansas. The town of Waxahachie lay on one of the many feeder paths that flowed in to the main trunk of the Chisolm Trail. Local cattleman Jeroboam D. Beauchamp had raised cattle prior to the Civil War, but only saw large returns afterward when he began to push his cows northward from Waxahachie to Kansas.

Trail bosses like Beauchamp rode mustangs, many of which were the offspring of the wild horses captured by the first pioneers to settle in the area, to round up the longhorns. The boss supervised an average of ten cowboys, a cook, and a horse wrangler, adventurous men—including whites, former African-American slaves, Mexicans, and South Americans—who pushed the herds north, allowing the cows to graze along for 10 or 12 miles a day, never pushing the cattle except to reach water. (Herds that ate and drank their fill rarely stampeded.) The trip averaged three months, and 2,500 head of cattle could be led to Kansas for 60¢ to 75¢ a head, far cheaper than shipping by rail.

One of the cowboys who pushed cattle along the feeder line that extended through Waxahachie claimed that he regularly drove 200 to 300 head of cattle straight through downtown, the dust and commotion forcing a temporary halt to business and court transactions. The cowboy Frank Olivaries had immigrated north from Argentina and taught many local men the traditional cow handling skills long associated with Argentinian ranching.

By the mid-1880s, Olivaries found the heyday of the cattle drives over. The invention and widespread distribution of barbed wire fenced in the great free plains, destroying the Chisholm Trail. Further, an 1885 Kansas quarantine law made it illegal for any Texas cattle to enter the state because of the persistent reoccurrence of Texas fever in midwestern cows. (Scientists discovered in the 1890s that the Texas fever was a microorganism and was transmitted by cow ticks. Longhorns had built up an immunity to the illness, but the disease was fatal to most other cattle.)

Although the cattle industry proved important to Waxahachie's economy immediately after the Civil War, the cultivation of cotton proved to have a far more significant impact. Before the war, less than 300 bales of cotton per year had been grown in Ellis County, but the war stimulated the planting of cotton. Women and the men in poor health or too old to fight in the war began to grow cotton, hoping to generate money with the only significant cash crop available to them. By the time the war ended in 1865, 2,000 to 4,000 bales of cotton were being grown in the county every year.

Despite the promise of cash on receipt, cotton still proved an unprofitable product for the people of Waxahachie to grow. The problem was not that the soil could not cope with such a demanding crop; in fact, the blackland prairie was so rich that it took nearly 50 years for the land to be exhausted, but that the

Bales of Ellis County cotton were gathered at yards to be weighed and prepared for shipment North. Notice the courthouse in the background and the cotton buyer representative sitting on a bale in the foreground.

transportation costs were so prohibitive; few people could afford to transport their cotton to markets. For example, in 1868, cotton grown in Ellis County had to be shipped overland to Bryan (almost 180 miles south) by mule or horse-drawn wagons at a cost of $5 to $12 a bale. The trip took four to eight weeks and could only be undertaken during the spring or fall when the prairie grass was abundant enough to support the animals. The farmers' only other option was to float the cotton bales down the Trinity River, a risky venture at best. When the weather was good, the Trinity varied between a small river and a barely flowing creek, but if a flatboat was caught in a spring thunderstorm, the rain and run-off swelled the river to a mighty raging wall of water, destroying everything in its path.

Despite the costs and hazards associated with transporting the crop, the farmers and planters around Waxahachie began growing more cotton after the Civil War ended because the price of the fiber continued to rise to levels unknown before the war. For example, during 1868, William H. Getzendaner, who had immigrated to Waxahachie after the war and made a living as a planter and lawyer, sold a bale of cotton in Galveston for $93 in gold, an incredible sum of money in the lean years of Reconstruction. Despite the good price cotton fetched, the county's farmers still grew corn and grain predominantly, but the coming of the railroad to the county in the 1870s foretold a shift in farm output.

On June 14, 1875, Waxahachie hosted a large barbecue, and over 4,000 residents came out to eat, celebrate, and watch the first spade of dirt be turned over for the new Tap Railroad being built that would link the city with the Houston and Texas

Central Railroad. The linkage reflected the increased prominence of the community in Texas's economy: Waxahachie incorporated as a city in 1871 and built a new, much larger courthouse in 1873, the third in little more than 20 years.

The county commissioners planned for the new courthouse to project an image of abundance and stability. Local builder A.C. Smith worked in cooperation with city officials to create a 60-foot-square, two-story building made from local stone at a cost of $40,000. Work began on the structure in the fall of 1870, and the builder brought in a hard yellow limestone, quarried only 2 miles east of downtown on the S.A. Clift homestead. By the building's completion in 1873, a simple but pleasing courthouse had emerged on the square. Eighty feet tall and topped with clocks facing each point of the compass, the legal house towered over the nearby commercial buildings and anchored the community. Horses surrounded the building on court days, tied to hitching posts. On many an afternoon, the boys who had accompanied their fathers downtown on business could be found dropping a worm in the pond on the courthouse grounds, hoping to catch a fish.

Irish immigrants were hired to do all the stone work and plastering on the new building. One of the foreign workers, John Solon, remained in Waxahachie and quickly became a prominent citizen. Working as a carpenter, builder, and brick mason, Solon opened the first brickyard in Waxahachie and built most of the brick and stone buildings in town. In addition to working on the new court of law, Solon built courthouses in Decatur and Weatherford—both similar in

The Nelson's home place represented a popular early architectural style common in the South during the Civil War and Reconstruction periods. The clean lines and simple construction provided excellent ventilation and ease in building.

style to Waxahachie's third courthouse. He also built the only stone house in Waxahachie, northwest of downtown on Solon Street (named in honor of John Solon). Solon built his home in 1889, hand cutting each stone from rock shipped on the Texas and Central Railroad from the Millsap quarry. Spending extra time on the horseshoe-shaped windows, the house cost $6,000 when completed—a large sum at the time, but one Solon could afford. The stonemason had divested his business interests and had begun to buy land. Soon, he was planting cotton and ranching, eventually owning more than 1,000 acres.

Solon was also one of the first Catholics in town, and he and his wife Mary Agnes were charter members in the newly formed Saint Joseph's Catholic Church. Having no children of their own, the Solons sponsored several baptisms and opened their home to every missionary priest who came through town. When an orphan train passed through Waxahachie, Solon and his wife took one of the boys on the train, an Irish child named Tom Gallagher, and raised him as their own. When John Solon died, Gallagher left Waxahachie, returned to his birth state of New York, and became a police captain.

The county had grown so large by the mid-1880s that a third, much larger courthouse was constructed in 1882. The 60-foot-square building was made from local stone at a cost of $40,000 and was entirely carved by Irish immigrants who settled in Waxahachie specifically to work on the structure.

Constructed in 1873 to meet the needs of an enlarged and prosperous population, the county's third courthouse was constructed entirely of local materials.

The Irish who came to work on the courthouse were not the only foreign immigrants arriving in Ellis County during the post-war years. The first significant European migration occurred in the county in 1873, the same year the new courthouse was finished. Hundreds of Czechoslovakians passed through Waxahachie in the 1870s, heading to neighboring Ennis where a large Slovak and Moravian population developed. In addition to the new Czech immigrants, dozens of Irish brick masons, who had come to the county to build the courthouse, stayed. The county's citizenry reflected a new and diverse dynamic—whites and freed blacks, Americans and Europeans—all living in a time of renewed peace and dedication to the pursuit of wealth and individualism.

Waxahachie had so many people interested in settling in the county that the city produced an information package, an early type of promotional and tourism brochure. In 1876, with the nation reunited politically once again, Waxahachie described the beauty and appeal of its lands to all. Towering oak, elm, hackberry, and pecan trees shaded homes, the pamphlet explained, while the two main water arteries, Waxahachie and Chambers Creeks, were lined with wild china, sweet gum, and honey locust trees and shrubs. The McCarney Rose grew wild everywhere and many homeowners used it as a hedge between fields. Land was still readily available, selling at prices as low as $3 to $8 an acre. Most farmers grew small grains, grasses, fruits, and vegetables, the brochure claimed, and honey was easily gathered and sold.

The brochure's creators highlighted many of Waxahachie's strengths, including its commitment to education. In 1869, the Northwest Conference of the Methodist Episcopal Church provided the funds to begin Marvin College, named in honor of Enoch M. Marvin, presiding bishop of the Trans-Mississippi Conference of the Methodist Episcopal Church, South.

Marvin College was the first school of higher education in Waxahachie. Named in honor of presiding Bishop Enoch Marvin, the Methodist school served the community from 1869 to 1884.

Waxahachie citizens subscribed approximately $15,000 in cash, land, and services to "erect suitable school buildings" and endow a first class school, college, or university. Emory Rogers deeded a total of 40 acres for $750 to the Methodist church trustees for the school's location (the property is located at the north end of College Street today)—land north of town that seemed remote at the time, but was quickly encroached by housing developments. Of the 40 acres deeded, Rogers donated 10 acres specifically for the creation of a college.

With land in place, church trustees began constructing a two-story building in the Gothic style that measured 70 feet by 50 feet. Resting on a 4-foot-thick rock foundation, the school building's materials were made by Rogers and Snyder brickworks from sand hauled out of Waxahachie Creek. A 13-foot-tall tower rose from the mansard roof and housed a bell donated by New York City merchants that could be heard for more than 5 miles (the bell is now housed in the Ellis County Museum). The first floor consisted of six recitation rooms and a 40-foot-square study hall that could seat 300 students. The entire second floor was devoted to a large chapel that seated 800 guests. The building cost $22,000 to construct and housed students until 1920 when it was demolished.

The school was innovative in its use of technology. It was one of the first colleges in the state to make use of the phonograph in the classroom, and it had a large observatory constructed on campus with a laboratory and a 9-foot equatorial telescope that had been ordered from Pike and Sons of New York.

Accepting students from the primer level to college degrees, Marvin College specialized in music, though it taught all the basic subjects. The college was considered by many to be one of the best in the state and attracted local students as well as children and youth from across the state—as many as 300 enrolled in any given semester, including Lee Ting, a student from China. The local newspaper editor claimed it was "soon to be the Cambridge of Texas."

Such optimism proved unfounded. Though the college offered a quality education, it was plagued by debts throughout its existence. Within a few years, the Methodist church had to sell the building and property. Several different individuals owned the property throughout the late 1870s, each continuing to operate a school in the building. By 1884, Marvin College ceased to exist. Mounting debts (the debt for the winter fuel bill of 1883 and 1884 alone was staggering; over 30 tons of coal had been needed to heat the campus buildings) and unpaid tuition bills forced the final closure of the school. The city purchased the land and buildings, and opened a public school in the structure, educating local children for the next 40 years.

Overcoming the national crisis of the Civil War and Reconstruction, Waxahachie stood poised in 1876 to assume its place as one of the leading agricultural counties in the nation. The growing population and increased emphasis on cotton brought a wealth and abundance to the community that it had not seen before nor would it know afterward. The years between 1877 and 1929 reflected the glory days of Waxahachie and gentility in living only possible with the affluence of cotton production during its years as king.

Cotton gins could be cheaply and easily constructed, and dozens sprang up around the county. Several operated in Waxahachie alone between 1877 and 1929, and cleaned and loosely baled hundreds of thousands of bales of cotton over the years.

4. When Cotton Reigned King

"Is he here yet?" The boy asked breathlessly after running to the train station from his house on West Main Street. "Nah, not yet," his friend replied, "but we'd better push to the front if we want to see him."

More than 200 people joined these two boys at Waxahachie's train station on February 28, 1916, and most of them were breathless, but from excitement rather than exertion. Automobiles lined the tracks as the city's townspeople waited for the arrival of the Detroit Tigers and their star player, Ty Cobb. The town's chamber of commerce had spent months and thousands of dollars advertising the city to Major League teams, and their hard work had paid off. The Detroit Tiger's manager had contracted with the city to host its spring training session in Waxahachie, but the players were apprehensive, expecting the little Texas town that none of them had ever heard of to be a "bush burg." Even the Tiger's manager had hesitated, only conceding to come to Waxahachie for spring training on the condition that the chamber of commerce spend $4,000 to improve the town's facilities.

The Tigers were surprised when they arrived. Instead of a backward western community, they discovered a thriving and educated city with luxurious accommodations, multiple amenities, and one of the largest and best baseball fields in the United States. Wanting to impress the team and hopeful that they might sign up to come again the next year, the chamber spent more than $6,000 on various structures.

The chamber contracted to refit the Rogers Hotel to improve its general appearance. Originally completed in 1912 on the grounds of the original Rogers House (built in 1856) and named in honor of Emory and Nancy Rogers, the hotel was the only lodging large enough to accommodate the entire team.

Turning the entire basement over to the Tigers, local builders installed a 20-foot-square hot mineral water pool (sulphur water was piped from a nearby deep artesian well, lending a distinct odor to the hotel the rest of the summer) for the team to "plunge" into after practice.

Additionally, builders installed four showers, two bathtubs, four rubbing tables, six dressing rooms, and 32 steel lockers in the basement alongside the pool.

The Rogers Hotel was built in 1912 on the site of the original Rogers House Hotel, which was operated by Emory and Nancy Rogers in 1856. The hotel represented the finest lodging available in Ellis County. Four stories tall, the structure had an al fresco *dining area on the roof, as well as an outdoor sleeping area.*

The city wanted to be sure the players had plenty of entertainment when they were not practicing, so they put in billiard tables for the team in the Rogers Hotel and converted two empty buildings downtown adjacent to the hotel into handball courts. For their ease and convenience, the chamber provided three automobiles for the team's exclusive use. If these amenities were not enough, the town reconstructed its baseball field, named Jungle Park (now Paul Richards Park in honor of a Waxahachie native who made good in the major leagues), because it was located on the grounds along the railroad tracks where the circus unloaded and housed its animals for its yearly performances. The field, larger than most Major League parks at the time, measured 412 feet to dead centerfield, was entirely enclosed, had a grandstand and bleachers, and was only a short 10-minute walk from downtown and the Rogers Hotel.

During the month that the Tigers spent training in Waxahachie, the Rogers Hotel brimmed to capacity. The team, coaches, sports writers, and loyal fans mingled in the hallways and on the mezzanine. They ate dinner together, sometimes in the dining room on the first floor, but if the weather was pleasant, the team and its fans ate on the roof in a specially constructed area for dining *al fresco*. Citizens from miles around gathered at the Rogers—mainly with the hope of seeing Ty Cobb—and most were lucky enough to not only see him but also

This photograph shows one of Waxahachie's cotton yards in the 1890s. The bales were brought to the yard from a nearby gin, weighed, and sat awaiting shipment by train to textile mills in the North or to Liverpool, England.

meet him. One sports writer said that Cobb had "shaken the hand of every man in Ellis County" during spring training.

The relationship proved agreeable in 1916. The night before the Tigers' last exhibition game, the chamber hosted a farewell dance. The next day, an estimated 3,000 fans showed up (the most people ever gathered for a sports event in the city to this point) to watch the Tigers beat the New York Giants 8 to 3. The team enthusiastically promised to return the next year, which they did, but things were never the same again.

By the spring of 1917, Waxahachie's fortunes were beginning to turn. It appeared inevitable that the United States would become involved in World War I, and the price of cotton and other agricultural products bounced from all time highs to miserable lows. The Tigers had witnessed the community in its heyday and now watched as the city began a slow decline. Most of the town's citizens did not realize that the years of seemingly endless wealth and prosperity were coming to an end—they could only look to their past success and imagine a similar future. In 1916, Waxahachie was a shining example of a New South city, apparently resurrected from the ashes of the Civil War and Reconstruction and fulfilling the prophecies of the New South Creed.

That creed had been originally prophesied in 1886 by a newspaper editor from Georgia named Henry W. Grady. Speaking at a gala dinner in New York, Grady preached the gospel of industry claiming the following:

> Old South rested everything on slavery and agriculture, unconscious that these could neither give nor maintain healthy growth. The New South presents a perfect democracy, a hundred farms for every plantation, fifty homes for every palace—and a diversified industry that meets the complex needs of this complex age.

The people of Waxahachie, well aware of Grady's speech and the movement it spurred among southerners, traced their success in the footsteps of the creed, even anticipating the set doctrine by more than ten years.

The movement toward diversification in the southern economy was well on its way years before Grady articulated the actions as a specific region-wide creed, and railroads proved the first means of diversification for southerners after the Civil War. In 1872, the Houston and Texas Central (H&TC) Railway considered routing its new tracks through Waxahachie, but the town refused to supply the required bonus. Not being a company that compromised, the H&TC simply chose a new route and built the city of Ennis, 20 miles east of Waxahachie, as a way station between Dallas and Houston. Quickly realizing their mistake, Waxahachie's businessmen funded a tap railroad track that linked the town with the H&TC—a pivotal decision that proved the first of many for the town's business sector. Never again did the community's leaders turn down a progressive commercial opportunity, and it was this forward thinking that carried Waxahachie beyond the average Texas town.

Cotton bales became a common site in Waxahachie's downtown area after the 1890s. The fiber reigned king in the county for more than 50 years and brought untold wealth to the community.

The coming of the railroad to Waxahachie marked the beginning of its climb to prominence and was probably the single most important reason why the town later proved so successful economically. The railroad line drew more people to the town, businesses sprang up, crops were easily shipped out, universities relocated, and social organizations were formed, all because the railroad came to Waxahachie. More and more, the community began to resemble the ideal New South town—an Old South agricultural emphasis mixed generously with manufacturing and commercial endeavors.

By the mid-1880s, Waxahachie serviced four different railroads—the H&TC; the Fort Worth and New Orleans; the Gulf, Colorado, and Sante Fe; and the Texas Central—for a combined 78 miles of track criss-crossing through Ellis County. The city and its surrounding neighboring towns—Midlothian, Ennis, and Milford—supported four banks, 270 merchants, 24 bricklayers, and 62 physicians. Land was still cheap and plentiful, improved acreage sold between $15 and $30 an acre and unimproved lands $10 to $20 an acre. The population had risen to more than 30,000 individuals with a fairly even distribution of males and females. Whites dominated, though, and there were less than 1,200 African Americans residing in the county in 1887 and only one individual claiming Mexican birth. Waxahachie was the largest town in the county with a population

In the late 1890s, a building boom erupted in Waxahachie, both expanding the commercial district and creating several new suburban neighborhoods. Notice the new stores and offices being built in the foreground of the courthouse.

Waxahachie businessmen invested in and built the cotton textile mill in 1901. The mill was one of only 13 that operated in the state during this period and could produce 7,500 yards of finished ducking or sheeting per day.

of 4,500 and the community was growing rapidly. The state census taker recorded more than 1,200 births in 1887 and 308 marriages. The death count was relatively small, only 402 deaths were recorded that year, and divorce was scarce, only 18 people filed for divorce. The town and the county prospered, and the Civil War and Reconstruction seemed in many ways only a distant memory.

Agriculture dominated the county's economy in the 1880s and the farmers still overwhelmingly grew cereal grains as their main crop. Fruits and vegetables were grown for table use and some were being shipped out via the railroad to markets in Dallas and Houston. Several men had begun harvesting honey—bee production proved significant in the area—and were selling it locally and to outside markets. Stock animals also contributed greatly to the economy and the Singleton farm near Mountain Peak (ten miles southwest of Waxahachie) was noted as one of the finest mule producing farms in the state.

Although the agricultural economy remained diversified in the 1880s, the county had already begun to show an increase in cotton production, made more feasible by the numerous railroad terminals and the Grange and Farmers' Alliances' efforts at reducing railroad shipping costs. By 1890, newspapers were reporting that Ellis County was one of the most significant cotton growing regions for its size in the nation.

The shift from cereal grains to cotton was gradual in the county, but once local farmers were lured by the high cash returns possible with cotton, they never looked back. So much cotton was planted in the county in the early 1890s that the acreage far surpassed the available labor supply. Waxahachie's mayor and leading businessmen formed a Board of Trade and laid out an advertising plan to attract new residents to move to the county and work in the fields harvesting cotton.

The advertising scheme consisted of publishing and distributing more than 50,000 pamphlets and running ads in numerous magazines across several southern states. The brochures highlighted the advantages of living in Waxahachie and cited several "interesting facts" about the county. The copy told of farm vacancies and the need for farm laborers, tenants, and sharecroppers.

Hundreds of people responded to the ads—most desperate, poor, and hoping to find a fresh start in what sounded like (at least in the pamphlets) God's promised land. Many whites, but far more blacks, moved to the county during the early 1890s directly as a result of the advertising scheme, and took up tenant and sharecrop farming. This demographic change reflected a similar increase across the southern states in the prevalence of sharecropping and tenancy and reinforced the move in Ellis County toward the exclusive production of cotton. A labor shortage was unique to Texas at the time, but the state's landowners solved the problem the same way landowners across the south were solving a similar problem—they had workers, but no cash to pay them for their labor.

Sharecropping and tenant farming came into use after the Civil War when landowners sought a means of hiring labor (often former slaves, but also poor whites, both of whom owned no land of their own) to farm on a non-cash basis. Sharecroppers, the very poorest of the farm workers, had nothing to offer the landowner but their labor. In return for tilling, working, and harvesting the crop, the owner supplied the cropper with supplies (seed, plows, livestock, groceries, and clothing) and a share of the crop, generally about half. Tenant farmers were hardly better off than croppers, but might offer the planter a mule, plow, or a line of credit at the local store. Tenants then might claim a larger share of the harvest,

This photograph, taken in 1914, reveals Waxahachie when it was still producing more cotton than any other region in the world.

commonly 75 percent of the crop. Such a system inevitably led to conflict and distrust. Landowners, looking to make the largest profits for the least amount of expense, demanded that their croppers and tenants plant cotton—the only cash crop during the post–Civil War period.

Tenancy and sharecropping spread across the south quickly and became increasingly popular in Texas in the 1890s as a means for cash-poor landowners to work their land. While ready cash was always a problem, Waxahachie's planters found the general labor shortage a far more significant block in their move toward increasing their cotton yields. The advertising scheme established by the Board of Trade solved the problem, though, and, with a marked increase in sharecroppers and tenant farmers, helped to move the county one step closer to its monocultural emphasis on cotton.

The men and their families that chose to sharecrop and tenant farm in Ellis County between 1890 and the late 1920s lived hard, subsistence lives. Most lived in run-down shacks, really just shanties where the wind whistled between the plank walls, and a family of five, six, or seven might experience happiness, sorrow, birth, and death within the space of one room. Privacy was a luxury that tenants and croppers could not afford—often insignificant because other concerns like finding enough food to feed all the children or adding cardstock to a pair of worn-out shoes took precedence.

These families began planting cotton in the spring, and it was almost always a family affair—they had little choice but to make their children and wives work alongside them. The men had signed contracts to work someone else's land, and the landowner inevitably chose to grow cotton. Not that the croppers or tenants would have argued in favor of grains or fruits or vegetables, because they too wanted the opportunity to make maximum cash profits. But growing cotton exclusively came with its own costs, mainly that it excluded the growing of anything else—vegetables for home consumption or grains for livestock—all that the workers had to buy on credit from local merchants. Such a system kept tenants and croppers in a perpetual state of debt peonage, never able to make

On one of the town's many cotton yards, over 15,000 bales of cotton could be lined up to await shipment.

Area farmers competed each year to bring in to the city's gins the first bales of cotton. Cash prizes were given by area merchants for the first bale and for the heaviest bale—a competition that had more than a few farmers trying to hide rocks in the midst of their cotton bales.

enough money from their share of the crop to pay their line of credit at the local store or save enough money to buy their own land.

Debt and poverty became a way of life for croppers and tenants across the south, including those families who farmed in Waxahachie. Most hung on, hoping that one year they would make enough money to pay their debts and put a little aside.

While spring found the farmers planting cotton, summer meant cultivation. Around Waxahachie, cotton harvesting began in late August—usually under the most intensely hot weather conditions of the year. Men, women, and children took to the fields from sun up to sun down and sometimes, as the harvest went along, they picked cotton by moonlight far into the night. The adults wore ducking bags 6 to 12 feet long that they strapped across a shoulder and dragged behind them down the rows. Many fashioned kneepads from old rags or bags to protect their legs as they crawled between the plants. Nothing could help their hands, though, and the cotton bolls dug deeply into their flesh, cutting, tearing, and callusing their hands as they labored hour after hour in the hot sun to harvest the cotton crop. The families ate their lunches in the fields, under the few scattered trees that might have sprung up along fence rows or in the shadows cast by the weighing wagons. Salt pork, cornbread, and water were staples, though sometimes a wife might rise early and make sugar water or even, occasionally, lemonade. Many a cropper mixed in a few watermelon seeds when he planted his cotton, and the whole family enjoyed a ripe melon during lunch freshly plucked from the vine.

A good cotton picker could pick well over 100 pounds of cotton per day, and each sack was weighed and inspected for size and cleanliness in the field. Temporary and migrant workers were paid by the pound daily, but tenants, croppers, and the owners of the land waited for payment till their cotton was prepared for market.

Once the cotton was harvested, it was taken by wagon to a nearby gin where the fiber was separated from the bolls and seeds, cleaned, and baled for shipment to markets. The gin yards were often crowded with farmers, testifying that they had the cleanest and heaviest bales, desperate to get the best possible price for their crop.

Whatever the prices, they hardly ever proved adequate in helping tenants and sharecroppers escape from debt. While the system held millions of southerners in privation, it still thrived, mainly because it proved profitable for the planters. Landowners in Ellis County found that growing cotton under the contract system brought them tremendous wealth, which encouraged them to dedicate even more acreage to planting cotton. The county grew more than 40,000 bales of cotton in the early 1890s; less than 20 years later, the area had become the largest cotton-producing county in the United States with annual outputs exceeding 180,000 bales.

More cotton production meant more profit and most of the county's landowners began to churn these profits into commercial endeavors. A wealthy elite class that owned large tracts of land emerged in the city, ran multiple businesses, invested in the community's future growth, and led the town in cultural and social entertainments.

Enterprising landowners began investing their profits in cotton gins almost immediately. Cheap and easily constructed, gins sprang up across the county; dozens of men located gins in Waxahachie alone and readied them to clean and bale local farmer's cotton. More expensive to build were cotton compresses, but by the early 1900s, Waxahachie hosted two compresses where farmers could bring their baled cotton and have it pressed into much more compact bales. These compresses were located near railroad terminals and allowed farmers to sell their cotton directly to buyers in New York, New Orleans, and Liverpool, England, thus eliminating the middle buyers and allowing for greater profits for farmers. Along with the gins and compresses, planters-turned-businessmen constructed cotton oil mills. Initially considered waste, cottonseeds were found to yield a quality oil (good for cooking, making soap, and mixing with animal feed) when pressed, and Waxahachie had as many as three separate cotton oil mills operating during the period.

The textile factory built in Waxahachie in 1901 was by far the largest commercial endeavor began as a result of the county's increased cotton production. Discussed as early as 1893, businessmen in the city could not muster enough local support for a mill until 1899, when Edwin A. DuBose spearheaded the move to build the mill.

DuBose arrived in Waxahachie in 1877 from Arkansas, initially residing with his uncle, one of the city's doctors. DuBose was 35 years old, an ambitious man having been seasoned in multiple Civil War battles. Immediately upon his arrival, DuBose began to make his mark in the town and was elected mayor by 1882. After serving six years in the city's highest-ranking political position, DuBose turned his attention away from civic endeavors and toward more purely capitalistic goals.

Believing that Waxahachie was short-changing itself by shipping its cotton bales north, DuBose proposed that local citizens fund a textile mill where local cotton could be finished into cloth. Finished cloth commanded higher market prices than did the raw bales of cotton. To garner support, DuBose traveled across Alabama and South Carolina, looking at various types of mills, making notes, and preparing to present his case to Waxahachie's businessmen.

When he returned, DuBose held a public meeting where he discussed the mills he had toured. He explained the various types of construction necessary to create a factory, and the looms and spindles that would have to be purchased to outfit it. He then described the kinds of workers that would be employed and the kinds of conditions they would work under. He had found that little villages

Another view of the city's cotton textile mill, the factory had at its peak 10,000 spindles and 200 looms. The decision to not only grow cotton, but also to try to manufacture it into a finished product, reflected the city's commitment to the New South creed.

Mill Village stood just south of Waxahachie's cotton textile mill. The hamlet was the self-contained city where the mill workers lived and supported a large boarding house, 24 small frame tenant houses, a church, a school, and an electrical generating plant. Wealthy locals often referred to the village dwellers as "lint heads," a derogative term that referred to the tiny bits of cotton lint that seemed to constantly cling to their hair and clothing.

formed around the mills and believed that generally the workers were well cared for—except, he explained, for the child labor he had witnessed. DuBose argued against the use of child labor in Waxahachie's mill, a common occurrence in mills across the United States where children as young as five and six were employed to change the intricate bobbins and shuttles on the looms (small hands made changing the mechanisms easier). Most of the town's businessmen were impressed and agreed with DuBose that a mill that produced heavy material like wagon sheeting and ducking might prove profitable.

Interested citizens formed a board of directors in January 1900 and began raising the $150,000 capital needed to start construction by creating 1,000 shares at $100 each. Within a few months, 104 Ellis County citizens had bought shares, enough investment to purchase 23 acres west of town along the Fort Worth and New Orleans Railroad. Before long, builders erected a factory and equipped it with 5,000 spindles and 150 looms. The board of directors supervised the building of an entire community on the south side of the mill for the operatives, which they named Mill Village. The little self-contained town consisted of a large

The mule streetcar system downtown. The streetcars serviced the busy downtown district for 20 years before the lines were electrified. The photograph illustrates the lively downtown business district in Waxahachie.

boarding house, 24 small frame tenant houses, a church, a school, and an electrical generating plant.

A siren blared for the first time at 7:00 in the morning on February 18, 1901, calling the more than 200 new mill workers to their first morning's work. William Howorth, brought all the way from England, supervised them. Twenty-five bales of cotton were fed into the machines at the beginning of each day. If all 150 looms were operating, the factory could produce 7,500 yards of sheeting or ducking a day.

At its peak, the Waxahachie Cotton Mill had 10,000 spindles and 200 looms. It was one of only 13 other mills in Texas and one of the largest in terms of capacity and production. Waxahachie's businessmen and leading citizens built the mill because they believed they were making a sound financial investment for themselves and for the future of their community. The decision to not only grow cotton, but also to try to manufacture it into a finished product, reflected the city's commitment to expansion.

Cotton manufacturing was not the only financial investment the people of Waxahachie were making for their future. Businessmen encouraged growth in several segments of the economy, always keeping an eye on the city's improving image. Waxahachie became one of the first communities in northern Texas to install telephones for home usage—a service petitioned and paid for by the townspeople.

More important to the city's growth was the move to bring electricity to the area. A native of Alabama, J.F. Strickland proved instrumental in electrifying Waxahachie. Arriving in the county right after the Civil War at the age of 16,

Strickland immediately went to work to improve his financial condition. He started by hiring out his labor and then began hauling freight for local businesses. Soon he saved enough money to open a gin. Within a few years, Strickland had engaged in the grocery business, both retail and wholesale, built an ice plant, and dabbled in real estate. While fostering his growing businesses, the entrepreneur also made time to serve as a city alderman and as the chief ax man in Waxahachie's newly formed fire department.

Ready to expand, Strickland began talking up electricity as the key to the making of a progressive city as early as 1887, but could not come up with the necessary capital to form a company until three years later. The opening of the Waxahachie Electric Company proved pivotal in the city's growth and Strickland's personal fortune. Both prospered as a result of the man's foresight.

The electrical power plant Strickland established in Waxahachie in the 1890s brought electricity to homes, city streets, and more importantly for the long-term success of the community, allowed multiple manufacturing concerns to establish themselves. Before long, a wholesale plant nursery opened, a creamery began producing butter and cheese, an electric gristmill began operating, and a carbonated soda bottling works company opened.

Saloons provided a popular form of entertainment for Waxahachie's early male citizens. Despite the country's move toward Prohibition, Waxahachie supported as many as seven different saloons prior to the turn of the twentieth century.

By 1900, Waxahachie's downtown business sector thrived. Three banks serviced the region, supporting local commercial enterprises as well as farmers expanding their landholdings and implements. Other businesses prospered too, including several grocery stores, two meat markets, two lumberyards, a half-dozen dry goods stores, a china and queen-ware shop, four confectionaries, two shoe shops, a tailor, and dozens of other assorted businesses. The city also had seven saloons, bars that had maintained a brisk business for many years despite the growing statewide movement toward Prohibition.

Although Waxahachie had developed a name for itself throughout the state and even nationally as a leading agricultural region, its leading citizens continually attempted to broaden its economic base by introducing new businesses and manufacturing concerns. The city's leaders were successful in their attempts, partly because they were in the forefront of a statewide move to expand growth through the scientific application of efficiency to city government. Incorporating as a city in 1871, Waxahachie's mayor and aldermen supported the creation of a commercial club and later a chamber of commerce, whose purpose was to attract the attention of manufacturers and labor to the city.

Both the Commercial Club and chamber of commerce proved effective at advertising the growing community, growth that fed on itself forcing other improvements in Waxahachians' standards of living. The city developed a water

Mule street cars were first established in Waxahachie in 1890. The mule-pulled cars connected the newly planned housing additions of the east and west ends with downtown. By the next year, a second streetcar company built track on a north-south line, making the entire city accessible by streetcar.

The electric interurban connected Waxahachie with Dallas to the north and Waco to the south, and is pictured here in 1915. Locals could then easily travel to the larger cities for a day of shopping.

system prior to 1900 that brought fresh water to citizens' homes, and waste disposal piping soon followed. Interested citizens organized a police department as well as a volunteer fire department. Many Texas cities developed these basic services for their citizens at the turn of the century, but few towns went as far as Waxahachie, particularly in its move to provide quality public transport.

O.E. Dunlap, who was born in Mississippi and traveled to Texas with his parents after the Civil War, first proposed a street railway line for Waxahachie in 1887. Dunlap, who had farmed after he came of age, had been elected justice of the peace for the county in 1877 and later decided to study law. After practicing as a lawyer for a few years, he was elected a county judge. After two terms as judge, Dunlap began investigating other possibilities for making money and believed that a system of public transportation would benefit him personally, but would also reflect the cosmopolitan nature Waxahachie was trying to project.

By 1890, Dunlap had formed a core group of investors, who chartered the Waxahachie Street Railway Company with a capital stock investment of $25,000. Laying several miles of tracks, the mule-pulled cars connected the newly planned housing additions of the east and west ends with downtown. The next year, a second streetcar company was formed that built track on a north-south line. Eventually, the two companies merged, fully connecting the downtown square

A sturdy interurban trestle, an electric interurban rail-line was headed up by local resident J.F. Strickland and completed in October 1913. The interurban carried only passengers and allowed businessmen, tourists, and shoppers an easy commute between Texas cities. Passengers disembarked downtown at the Rogers Hotel, and could board an electric streetcar and reach any point in the city in a matter of minutes.

with outlying houses, businesses, and schools. Racing along at seven miles an hour, the cars serviced the city from dawn until dusk and cost 5¢ per fare. The mule streetcars were a regular fixture in Waxahachie for almost 20 years.

Outdistanced by technology, the mule streetcars were replaced in 1912 by the creation of an electric street railway system, a change that hardly made a ripple in the city because it coincided with the expansion of the electric interurban line into Waxahachie. As early as 1906, interurban railway lines were being built in northern Texas, connecting cities like Denison and Sherman with Fort Worth and Dallas. The lines carried passengers only and ran multiple times per day, representing an early version of a long distance commuter system.

J.F. Strickland, whose interests in developing electrification uses had led him into the building of electric rail systems, formed the Southern Traction Company and proposed connecting Waxahachie with Dallas to the north and Waco to the south. By October 1913, his vision had become a reality. Now, businessmen, tourists, and shoppers could easily commute between Texas cities. Serviced by an outside line, passengers could disembark downtown at the Rogers Hotel, board an electric streetcar, and travel easily to any point in the city.

Waxahachie experienced tremendous growth and prosperity during the period between 1890 and 1910. The city's agricultural prominence coupled with its commitment toward economic diversification attracted many new citizens, who brought greater wealth and diversity with them.

The actual city limits expanded during this period. A building boom began in 1900 and continued almost uninterrupted for over 20 years. An enlarged

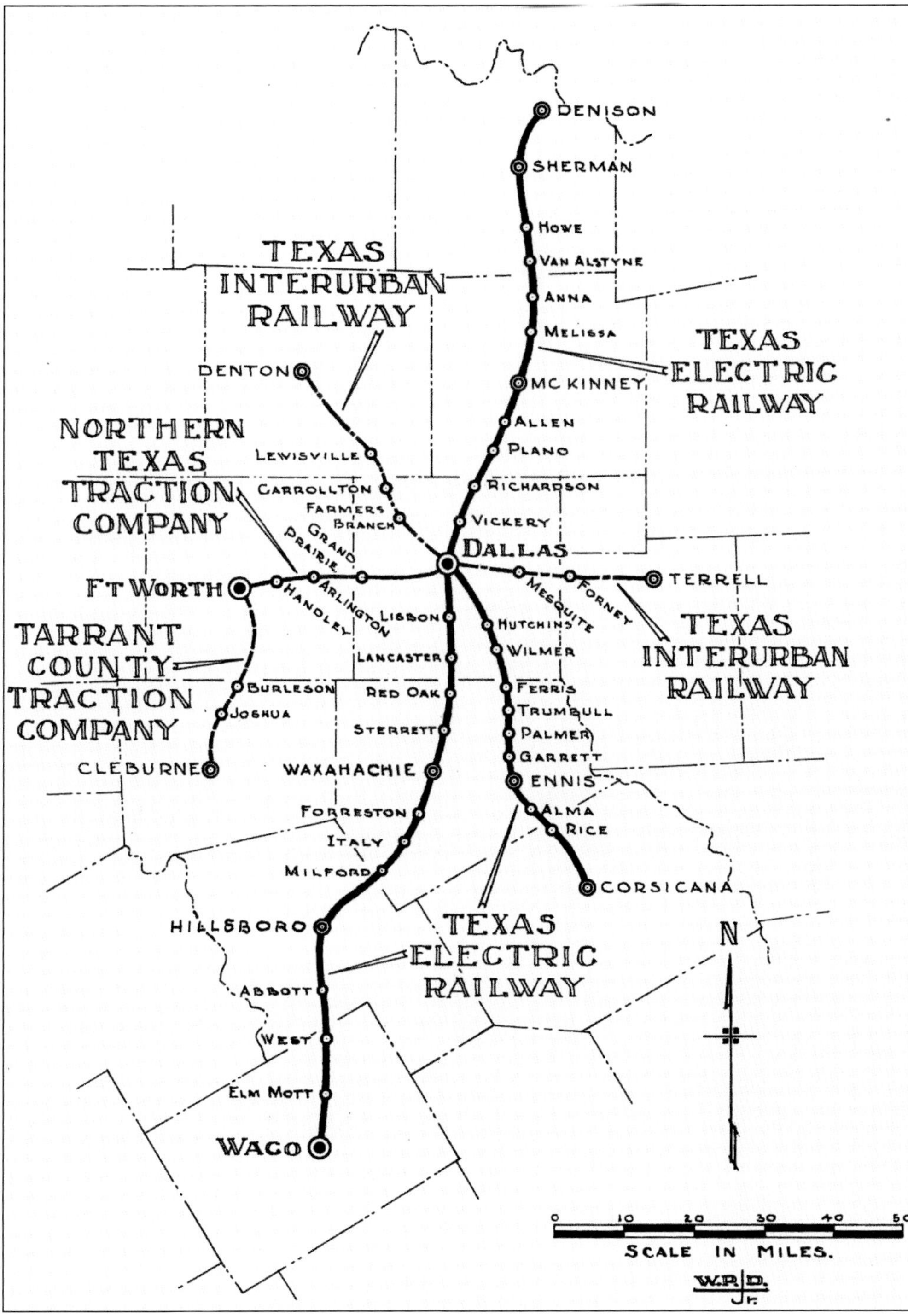

A map of the interuban's route, the electric passenger train plied its way between Dallas and Waco until 1948 when service was finally ended. Many of Waxahachie's leading female citizens boarded the train in the morning, planning to have lunch in downtown Dallas.

and expanded downtown sector, many new public buildings, and several upscale housing additions resulted from the communities' increased wealth and social importance.

The city's fourth and final courthouse proved to be one of the most significant architectural additions during the period. Controversial from the beginning, the cost, need, and choices in site location caused citizens to erupt into bitter debates, but after months of arguing, the cornerstone was laid on July 4, 1895, with thousands attending the ceremony and barbecue picnic that followed.

Although architect James Riely Gordon designed the courthouse, he never provided any services to the county. It was his business associate, Otto Kroeger of San Antonio, who sold the county Gordon's plans and initially served as the structure's contractor. Caught in the inter-city politics surrounding the courthouse, Kroeger was dismissed as contractor and the county hired the Fort Worth architect Marshal Sanguinet to construct the massive building.

With a cost exceeding $175,000, Ellis County's courthouse stands 9 stories tall and has more than 23,000 square feet of courtrooms and offices. It is constructed entirely of Texas materials—the exterior created from 160 carloads of Burnett

This is an elevated view of the county's courthouse, c. 1910. The Romanesque structure was completed in 1897. Designed by J. Reily Gordon and built entirely of Texas materials, the courthouse cost $175,000 to construct. It has recently been renovated and restored to its turn-of-the-twentieth-century glory.

This photograph taken from one of the courthouse's many arched porticoes reveals a bustling street scene. Notice the fine dresses and hats worn by many of the women shopping on the downtown square.

County red granite and 100 carloads of Pecos red sandstone from the Quito Rock Quarry in Ward County. The building retains its original copper gutters and downspouts and many of the furnishings designed by Gordon and Sanguinet specifically for the courtrooms.

The "Richardsonian Romanesque" courthouse is majestic from a distance, an architectural style made popular by architect H.H. Richardson. Standing squarely in the middle of the downtown section, the building can be seen from miles around. Many a farmer aimed his wagonload of cotton for the courthouse after it was completed in 1897, keeping one eye fixed on the tall clock tower and the other on the graceful arches that flank each side of the structure. The building's beauty and symmetry is stunning from afar, but it is the intricate sculptures that grace the courthouse's exterior that have attracted the most attention and speculation.

A series of intricately carved stone faces grace each of the four porch capitals, ranging from the sublime to the grotesque. Legend has it that German itinerant stonecarver Harry Herley fell in love with the local girl Mabel Frame, whose grandmother operated the boarding house where he resided while sculpting all the courthouse's exterior ornamentation. Herley loved Mabel Frame dearly,

Completed in 1905, the Nicholas P. Sims Library has served Waxahachie for almost 100 years. The ornate structure houses a lyceum on the second floor, accessible by an ornately carved staircase of Carrera marble.

the myth proclaims, but she did not return his love. The beautiful likenesses of Mabel portrayed on the stone porticoes soon turned into demons. Time and the dwindling love affair are portrayed as one walks around the courthouse.

While a lovely legend, there is no factual basis to the story. Harry Herley is credited with being the master carver for the Waxahachie project, but more than likely, he carved only a portion of the portraits and supervised several other carvers, all of whom worked for Theodore Beilharz, a master stonecarver in Dallas. The carvings were probably made in Dallas at the Beilharz yard and shop and shipped to Waxahachie in their finished condition, ready to mount. No connection between Herley and Frame can be documented and soon after the carvings were finished, Herley married a woman named Minnie Hodges. Despite the lack of evidence, the legend regarding the courthouse portraits survives and adds an extra element of romance and intrigue to an already significant architectural landmark.

The courthouse was not the only public structure built during the period. Fort Worth architect S. Wemyes Smith designed the town's library and lyceum, a neoclassical building with stylized Doric columns. Nicholas P. Sims, a local farmer, provided for the original structure in 1905 in his will, and the building is named in his honor. The building sits on the grounds of an early school and was given to the city by W.H. Getzendaner, a local banker and landowner. Additions have been added to the library, an east wing added in 1958 (donated by Mr. and Mrs. W.H. Larkin) and the west wing, which was constructed in 1966 (by local inventor J. Harry Phillips, who invented the red-headed concrete anchor). The lyceum, located on the second floor, has been perfectly preserved and can be reached by a double stairway of Carrera marble.

The Rogers Hotel, located downtown on the site of the Rogers family's original homestead, was also built during this period. Completed between 1912 and 1913, the four-story structure replaced an earlier hotel that had recently been destroyed by fire. Costing $100,000 to build, the lodging was considered to be the finest in all Ellis County. The hotel had 60 guest rooms, and each room had a sink with hot and cold running water. Thirty of the rooms had private baths, and most were equipped with telephones controlled by a central operator and switchboard that could then connect the guests with an outside line.

"Mattie, don't touch anything," her mother said. Mrs. Kimball had heard that the newly opened Rogers Hotel was hiring and, in need of money, she had come to town to apply for a job. Bringing her young daughter with her was probably not the best idea, but she had no one who could watch her.

"Ma'am, I can talk with you now," the hotel manager called out to Mrs. Kimball. "Mattie, sit right here and don't move a muscle—you hear me?" said her mother. "Yes, ma'am," replied Mattie.

For a while after her mother left, Mattie was as good as she could be. The hotel's entry was beautiful and there was so much to see. The tiled floors made intricate patterns, and the ceiling was embossed and heavily ornamented. The wood on the walls and furniture glistened, and everything was so shiny. Mattie watched as bellhops helped lodgers into the hotel; some drove up to the front door in cars and others came from the electric interurban rail line. Its main terminal was located in an annex on College Street on the east side of the Rogers Hotel.

The hops showed the guests to the front desk and took their suitcases through to the back. The guests signed their names in a large book (Mattie knew it was their names they were writing because the clerk said, "sign your name here, please") and then were shown the way up the big staircase that wound above the desk. But she wondered why their cases went to the back—"wouldn't they need them?" she wondered.

After a while, her curiosity became too great. "I'll only be gone a minute," she thought, as she hopped off the chair where she had been sitting. Following one of the hops who was carrying a large trunk, Mattie watched as he approached something that looked like a cage.

"What is that?" Mattie asked. The hop looked at her curiously, but then replied, "It's the freight elevator, kid."

The hotel was even more interesting in the back, if not so beautiful. Employees busily came and went through doors that led in every direction, and the elevator kept going up and down. Some men carried trays of food, while women dashed around with towels and sheets.

Forgetting all about her mother, Mattie was engrossed with the activities all around her. Turning into one door, she saw small bales of cotton on the floor and piles of the fiber on tables. In one corner, a display of pots and pans sparkled. Mattie had walked into the Sample Room, an area in the hotel designed so that local cotton growers could bring in examples of their crop for visiting buyers to preview. Additionally, traveling salesmen selling to stores in the town could display their wares, such as the pots and pans, so that the ladies could come through the room while they were shopping downtown and see the latest merchandise available.

Turning around, Mattie wound her way back through the service area and opened another door that led into the kitchen. Cooks were lined up; some working over large stoves, while others were cutting and dicing vegetables. White plates were stacked on one end of a counter and one of the workers was busily arranging food on two plates. He then covered the food with two shiny little pots, placed the plates on a tray, and took the tray to another little cage. The cook alerted a waiter that his tray was headed up stairs.

"Where is that food going?" Mattie asked the man in the white apron.

The cook looked at the little girl, assuming that she was the daughter of a guest. "Well," he replied, "you can order food to eat in your room . . . I get it ready and put it in that dumbwaiter, then a waiter brings it right to your room . . . Ask your Daddy—maybe he will let you order room service while you're here."

"Now, why don't you get on back to the dining room," said the cook.

Mattie looked at the man. His face was as dark as the dirt on the farm where her daddy grew cotton for Mr. Getzendaner. Mattie looked around. All the men and women in the kitchen had faces as black as night, but most of their cheeks glistened with sweat from the steam billowing into the air from several large pots.

The cook motioned toward a door at the far end of the kitchen and Mattie walked through the crowded room, twice stopping as workers pushed in front of her, one carrying a large tray and another a big bowl with a wooden spoon barely visible over the top. Upon reaching the door, she looked back once more at the commotion and then pushed through into the dining room.

Unlike the kitchen, the café was filled with white people. Four ladies in fancy hats were sitting at one end of the room drinking from delicate little cups. At another table, two men were laughing, and one had a little bit of butter and cornbread dangling from his mustache. Mattie climbed up on to one of the chairs and looked at the menu sitting on the table. She recognized only a few of the words—turkey, mashed potatoes, Texas yams—but she had never seen most of the other words on the menu, let alone eaten the foods.

The menu card was filled from top to bottom, each of the listings lettered in fancy script. The food offered represented the fine dining available at the Rogers Hotel during its peak period. Guests could begin their meals with grenadine cocktail or a canapé Lorenzo and continue to nibble on English cheese sticks, native celery, and queen olives. Main entrées included a medallion of sole dressed in a hollandaise sauce with *pomme noisette*, croustades of sweetbreads, and *petite pois* on the side, or if the diner preferred something other than beef, they could order a roasted turkey with stuffing and cranberries, mashed potatoes, and candied yams. The entrée was followed by a *salade epicure* and several cheeses with a choice of punch, tea, or coffee to drink. Deserts rounded out the meal and included a choice of plum pudding, hot mince pie, or toasted wafers *café noir*. To freshen the mouth, the waiter ended the meal by handing out after-dinner mints.

A waiter soon spotted Mattie sitting by herself and shooed her out of the dining room. Walking back through the lobby, she slowly climbed the stairs to the mezzanine, running her hand across the smooth wooden banister. Looking out from the second floor, Mattie could see the two telephones in the entry, tucked underneath the main staircase. Climbing the stairs again, she went higher and higher until she finally reached the top.

Opening the door at the end of the hallway, Mattie walked out onto the roof of the hotel. There to the left (on the west side) was another dining area. A tall pergola stretched the length of the building, and tables and chairs were neatly lined up underneath it. Flowers and pots of small trees surrounded the dining area, lending the impression that the visitor was eating in a secluded garden. At one end, a wooden dance floor was laid out and Mattie could imagine the lovely women in their dresses floating as their partners led them out on to the floor, a band playing underneath the moon and stars at night.

The Rogers Hotel was the finest hotel in the county. It sported a rooftop garden for diners who wanted to enjoy the scenery and fine food. Across the walkway on the roof, guests could sleep outdoors on cots erected by the hotel.

The stately Rosemont was built by local grocery man John H. Moffett in 1894. The home, credited to J. Riely Gordon, the same architect who designed the courthouse, has 20 rooms and 4 stories and cost $12,000 to construct.

The other half of the roof (the east side) had rows of cots in a line like soldiers. It was the outdoor sleeping area, and many of the hotel guests preferred sleeping on the roof under tents of mosquito netting in the summer months. Mattie crossed the roof floor, passing by another dumbwaiter (that brought the food to the *al fresco* dining area from the main kitchen on the ground floor) and headed for the cots. Laying back on one, she looked up into the brilliantly blue sky and watched as two mockingbirds chased a large black crow away from the nest they had built in one of the many large plants growing in pots on the roof.

"There you are," Mattie heard her mother say.

Mattie looked up and saw that her mother was angry. "I was just looking at the birds Momma," she said, but she knew that she was in trouble.

Her mother took her hand and led her back toward the door she had exited only a few minutes before. Looking out across the roof, Mattie could see the clock on the courthouse and to its side, the sculpted eagle that flew perpetually along the roof ridge.

"Oh Momma, come look," Mattie pleaded.

Mrs. Kimball relented, as captured by the sight as her daughter. Looking out from the hotel's roof, the two could see the downtown streets and the people bustling about. The courthouse lawn was crowded with children. The boys were running about playing with hoops and sticks, and a few were chasing each other playing "kick the can." The girls gathered in small groups, some showing off the new dresses their mothers had made them. In the midst of the children, the newly erected Confederate monument seemed to rise from the ground, the soldier at parade rest, but with a proud and defiant look in his eyes. The statue, funded by the local chapter of the United Daughters of the Confederacy, had occasioned a grand memorial ceremony the year before, and the city square had been packed as citizens came from all over the county to visit and retell war stories.

New construction stood alongside the more established commercial buildings downtown. The square had expanded; businesses overflowing onto several adjacent streets and even down toward the train tracks south of town. Mattie could see the cotton gin where her father took their cotton each fall and the two new warehouses being built beside it.

While Waxahachie's building spree enlarged the downtown area and added significantly to the city's public buildings, it also affected the private home market. Reflecting the increased wealth, the city's financial elite created new "suburban" housing areas to the south, east, west, and eventually the north of downtown and competed in the creation of neighborhoods filled with vernacular and popular house styles. For example, land speculators plotted out the Bullard Addition, south of Waxahachie Creek, and the West End Addition, west of downtown, just before the turn of the twentieth century. The areas were advertised as "premier living," removed from the business sections, but easily reached by the city's mule street cars. Many leading citizens bought lots in the new additions and built multi-storied Victorian and neoclassical revival homes.

Though plainer than Rosemont, the P.W. Watson home reflected the varied architectural types represented in Waxahachie during its building boom. The large house and extensive grounds combined city living convenience with enough acreage to plant a large garden and keep a few milk cows. Notice the cotton planted beside the home.

John H. Moffett built the finest home in the Bullard Addition at 701 South Rogers Street in 1894 and named it Rosemont. Attributed to J. Riely Gordon, the same architect who designed the courthouse, the 20-room, 4-story home cost $12,000 when it was constructed. The house is graced by wide, two-story verandas, ten fireplaces, jog awn brackets and capitals, three chimneys with corbelled caps, a round projecting bay capped with a pressed metal onion dome and finial, and roof cresting. Original outbuildings still stand on the property and include a well house with a mansard roof and a brick greenhouse. Moffett was an early settler in the area and prospered quickly. He owned hundreds of acres in Ellis County and in two other Texas counties. Divesting, he used his profits from growing cotton to buy a grain mill, cotton gin, and an ice manufacturing plant.

The West End Addition, west of downtown and anchored by Getzendaner Park, contained some of the town's largest and most architecturally interesting homes. Oscar E. Dunlap, an Ellis County judge from 1882 to 1886 and later the president of Citizens Bank, built the Dunlap House at 1203 West Main Street in 1891—one of the first homes to be established in the West End. The house was valued at $3,000 and was chosen from *Shoppell's Modern Houses*, a magazine published during the period that featured the up-to-date homes for America's financially discerning homeowners. The house was built in the Queen Anne

O.E. Dunlap, a county judge and bank president, built one of the city's finest homes in the West End Addition near Getzendaner Park in 1891. The family chose the house plans from a national magazine called Shoppell's Modern Houses *and had a local builder construct the home for $3,000.*

One of the many city services offered to Waxahachians prior to 1900, mail carriers lined up to have their photograph taken before their mail run. Prior to the use of mail carriers, citizens made weekly or monthly trips into town to collect their mail from the post office or relied on neighbors to gather it for them.

style with an asymmetrical façade, corner tower, patterned shingle siding and decorative woodwork on the porches, eaves, and gables. Dunlap purchased the lot in the newly created addition, an area being developed in a manner consistent with the ideas of the garden suburb movement. The lot was large and was situated near the garden-ellipse where the mule-drawn streetcars turned around, taking passengers back toward the downtown sector.

Further west on North Grand Street, two of the city's grandest homes sit side-by-side. Originally built in 1895 for H.W. Trippet, president of the Waxahachie National Bank, the Queen Anne house at 209 North Grand Street is one of the city's most imposing homes. The house, evidently meant to serve as a visual symbol of its builder's financial success, is one of the largest houses in town in terms of square footage and height. One of the house's most noticeable features is the corner tower, rising from the attic level with an elongated, bulbous roof and a decorative finial. Large two-story galleries encircle the house, curving around two sides and encompassed by the main hipped roof, lend further size and depth to the overall structure. Hosea Trippet built the ten-room house after having purchased all the stock in his father's dry goods store, and the new home was a testimonial to his recent business ventures. Unfortunately, he overextended himself. Trying desperately to hold onto the house, Trippet finally sold out and

Joshua Chapel, the African Methodist Episcopal Church in Waxahachie, was designed by William Sydney Pittman and built in 1917.

the house passed through another's hands when it was finally purchased by R.W. Getzendaner, a leading businessman and planter in the city, in 1910 for $12,500.

Next door at 203 North Grand Street sits one of the city's finest examples of the neoclassical revival style. Built in 1903 by M.B. Templeton, a county judge and prominent businessman, the house reflects a popular architectural style in Texas between 1900 and 1910. Based on a four square plan, two-story frames embellished with double-storied porches rise high, recalling hundreds of southern plantation homes found in the Deep South states.

Dozens of similarly grand homes are scattered throughout Waxahachie's older streets—many in formerly defined neighborhoods that have now lapsed into lower income areas. The East End, east of downtown, is one such area. Although several large homes reflect the city's wealth and a planned "white" and elite neighborhood, the portion of town east of the courthouse that adjoined the East End subdivision became a separate and segregated enclave in the 1890s for African Americans. Moving east along Main Street, small houses built in the "shot-gun style"—sometimes no more than two or three rooms deep and all aligned, where you can look through the front door straight out the back door—were built no more than a stone's throw away from grand Victorian showcases. Now the houses seem to blend together, contrasting in their obvious wealth differentiation, but when they were originally built, they represented very separate areas. One neighborhood for whites and, though within sight, another for blacks.

Similarly, East Main Street developed as a separate business district with grocery and drugstores, tailors, and restaurants specifically designated for black citizens and apart from the "white" businesses. The James Funeral Home was one of the longest lasting, African-American-owned businesses that operated during the period, and it was located along the 400 block along East Main Street. The funeral home occupied only the main floor, though, and the Pythagoras Lodge #87 used the upper floor. Members of the "black" Masonic Lodge, as it was known in town, represented the city's most elite African Americans, both businessmen and a few landowners.

Most African Americans in Waxahachie occupied small houses off East Main Street, structures that have only recently been deemed architecturally significant, significant because they represent the vernacular style commonly associated with African-American Texans at the turn of the twentieth century. Of greater significancc, however, is Joshua Chapel—one of the few black churches that developed in Ellis County during the period.

Newly freed slaves gathered outside of Waxahachie in 1866, founding the first African Methodist Episcopal (AME) Church in the county. While this first

Oak Lawn educated the town's African Americans in segregated facilities. The school, located on Wyatt Street, sat next to the Joshua Chapel.

effort failed, ten years later, enlarged by more members, a second AME Church purchased a plot on Aiken Street (east of downtown) and began to construct a church building that they named Joshua Chapel after their first pastor, Joshua Goins, who is recognized as the father of African Methodist Episcopalism in Texas (he organized 41 churches and built 14 church buildings during his life).

For almost 40 years, African-American Waxahachians worshipped in the small structure they had originally built in 1879, but with attendance mounting, they eventually planned to build a new church. Laying the cornerstone in 1917, the two-story, red brick structure—simply renamed Joshua Chapel—had been designed by William Sidney Pittman, son-in-law of Booker T. Washington and Dallas's leading African-American architect from 1913 to 1925.

The new building seated 400 people and was, most of the time, filled to capacity. Not only did the church have a membership of more than 300 people, Joshua Chapel was the center of African-American life in Waxahachie. School plays, programs, and graduations were held in the church. Community meetings transpired and clothing drives were organized in the sanctuary. The congregation began the Penn Park Little League for the boys who wanted to play baseball, and planned and built an apartment complex for lower income African Americans.

Joshua Chapel truly formed the nucleus of the African-American community, but standing next to it (both literally and figuratively) sat their segregated school,

The Oak Lawn school was located on Wyatt Street. The segregated school educated the city's African-American youth for more than 80 years. This c. 1915 photograph shows a few of the school's students.

This is Oak Lawn Academy's first graduating class. Two of the men pictured went on to earn college degrees and then returned to work in the school.

Oak Lawn Academy. Opening in 1887 as an elementary school for the town's African-American children, the school expanded over the years and graduated its first class with only four students in 1896.

George Murray Munchas was one of the hundreds of African-American children in Waxahachie who received a fine education at Oak Lawn. Born in 1887, Munchas's parents had been slaves in Alabama and had fled the state by horse after the Civil War. The family fared well in Texas, and Munchas's father was one of the first black men to own land in the county—a social position, even in the days of Jim Crowe, that separated the Munchas children from many of the other African-American children in the area. All of the Munchas boys graduated from Oak Lawn, and George went on to college and eventually obtained a medical degree.

Other children, ones like Etoy Cleaver Sapp, had to work a lot harder at getting their degrees from Oak Lawn, but all the children valued the excellent education they could get at the school. Although Sapp was the valedictorian of her class in 1919, she said that she never managed to make it on time for the start of the school term. "It was always after Thanksgiving," she said, "until then we was always too busy choppin' cotton." Sapp said she made about $1 a day picking cotton as a child, but much preferred working math problems or diagramming sentences on the board at school.

Trinity University relocated to Waxahachie in 1901. The university's many facilities, including this chemistry lab, offered a state-of-the-art education to the youths who were educated on the campus.

Chester Childs moved to Waxahachie in 1904 and began school at Oak Lawn shortly afterward. He later recalled that the school consisted of a white frame building (at that time) with two rooms downstairs and two rooms upstairs, and was heated by a large cast iron coal heater. He studied history, algebra, physiology, geometry, Latin, and English, but Childs most enjoyed playing on the school's baseball team and wearing the navy blue uniforms with white trim on the seams.

While Oak Lawn was the only school for African Americans in Waxahachie (the school system remained rigidly segregated well into the late 1960s), white children had several choices. By the 1890s, the public school system was well developed and several private schools operated in different parts of the town. Additionally, Trinity University, a co-ed four-year college, relocated to the city in 1901. Located on grounds north of downtown, the Presbyterian university serviced the region's higher educational needs for more than 40 years.

Coinciding with Trinity's relocation to Waxahachie, the Shelton Opera House opened in 1902. Accommodating as many as 1,000 people at a time, the entire theater was illuminated by tiny white lights. The large stage could hold a complete acting troupe, and the house hosted several companies a year. The Curtiss Comedy Company played at the theater the night it opened and had the large crowd crying with laughter.

On one occasion, a temperance speaker named Soule Sherrill passed out handbills declaring that he would be lecturing on the "evils of drink" at the opera house. Adults could hear him speak from experience—he was a reformed drunk after all—for only 50¢ while the children would be admitted for free. A group of citizens gathered to hear his speech, but later joked that on the night of the lecture, Sherrill was so drunk that he could not make it up the stairs to speak.

V.H. Shelton, owner of the opera house, was well pleased with his investment, despite the occasional problem like Sherrill's lecture. Having emigrated to Waxahachie from Arkansas in 1886, Shelton had engaged in several businesses, including the running of a drugstore. He also held stock in the Lake Park Street Railroad Company and the Waxahachie Cotton Seed Oil Mill. Shelton was a prominent member of the city's social circles. A wealthy businessman and the owner of more than 700 acres, Shelton was well admired for his "genial manner, good judgment, and strict fidelity to his duties." He operated the opera house until it burned to the ground in 1912.

While social engagements had been held in the city before the arrival of the Shelton Opera House or Trinity University, they were marked with a decidedly refined air afterward. Many of the university's faculty became mainstays at social entertainments and backyard musicals. One group in particular, the Lonestar Band, formed as a direct result of the cultural uplifting Trinity's faculty brought to the city.

The Lonestar Band was comprised of Waxahachie's finest young musicians. Marching in President Woodrow Wilson's inauguration parade in 1917 was the band's crowning achievement.

The Lonestar Band, made up of high-school-age boys who wanted to learn a musical instrument, began practicing in private homes in 1910. Norris Crawford, head of music at Trinity University, taught the boys and secured subscriptions from local merchants to offset the band's expenses—gold plated instruments, practice halls, lights, and blue serged uniforms. The band performed until 1928, entertaining audiences locally at Getzendaner Park, the Chautauqua Auditorium, and on the lawn of Sims Library. Their greatest moment of glory, however, came in 1917 when they marched in the presidential inauguration parade for Woodrow Wilson.

The young people of Waxahachie led active social lives and hosted varying types of parties. One get-together, dubbed a "progressive conversation" party, became the rage among the younger set during the period. Most of these parties began with a dinner—if hosted during the warmer months, dinner was served outside and usually included hand-cranked ice cream—and conversation following. The party's host distributed a different topic to each person, who then had two minutes to talk about their subject. The best speaker, as voted by the other partygoers, received a cake (or a similar prize). Popular topics included the weather, what

Department stores became popular in Waxahachie at the turn of the twentieth century, as they did across the country. These male and female sales clerks posed in front of one of Waxahachie's department stores during their "green tag sale." Women often spent the morning shopping and then had tea or coffee and a sweet in the store's coffee shop.

One of the cheapest means of entertainment, the county's youth always enjoyed an afternoon swimming in one of the area's many creeks. The Matthews children paused during their fun for a photograph.

constitutes a fascinating gentleman, old maids, matrimony, Shakespeare, women's rights, whether marriage was a successful institution, and Chautauqua. These topics and the very nature of the party reflected the current issues that young people faced at the turn of the twentieth century: leaving childhood behind, becoming adults, and understanding the shift occurring, changing the world from a strictly patriarchal society to one that might offer more equality for women in marriage and in work.

These same young people, and many of their parents, organized and joined dozens of social and self-improvement clubs during the period. A literary society sprang up in the early 1880s for both men and women, but as time passed, the clubs tended to separate into strictly male or female organizations. The men of the city joined Masonic lodges and rotary clubs and the women formed Shakespeare clubs (to study Shakespeare's works), formed the White Rose Club (to study music), initiated a chapter of the United Daughters of the Confederacy, and a Garden Club. These organizations remained rigidly segregated, but African Americans in the city formed similar clubs: Masonic lodges for men and church societies for women.

These organizations, while social in many aspects, also had an element of seriousness about them, but there were other types of social activities in Waxahachie between 1900 and 1920 based purely on enjoyment, and included a far wider circle of people, both young and old, rich and poor.

Shaw's Plunge, an outdoor swimming hole, was one of Waxahachie's favorite recreations. People from miles around came to swim in a dammed section of Waxahachie Creek, paying 15¢ a piece to swim or, if they needed to rent a swimsuit, 25¢. A grove of trees provided shade, and picnic tables were available to swimmers who bought refreshments: hamburgers, hot dogs, candy, and cold drinks could all be purchased. Although the food and conversation were enjoyed, the people mainly came for the swimming. A platform had been anchored out in the middle of the creek and there were also diving boards and a mud-sliding bank. For many years, friends and families met at Shaw's when they wanted to have a little fun and forget the heat.

Meeting at Shaw's was relatively easy, despite the fact that it was located several miles northeast of town near a little community called Lone Elm. By the time the pool was up and running, many of Waxahachie's citizens owned automobiles. The new-fangled contraptions first hit the city's streets in 1908. John Spaulding, a local furniture maker and casket builder, owned one of the first automobiles in Waxahachie, but many more soon followed as citizens bought cars by the hundreds during the next decade. Texas had been registering and regulating automobiles for one year when Spaulding bought his, so he was restricted by the state to driving 8 miles an hour in residential areas and 18 miles an hour out in the country. If Spaulding met an oncoming horse or wagon, he had to pull over and kill his engine so as not to frighten the animal, a problem most serious (so the state assumed) if women were in or around the wagons. The automobiles also had to be outfitted with a bell that could be heard from 300 feet and if operated during the dark, the driver had to mount or hold a lantern so that others might see the automobile approaching.

The coming of the automobile to Waxahachie marked the growth and changes that occurred in the city between the end of the Civil War and the beginning of the Great Depression. Their presence, and soon their abundance, reflected the new century and the technological presence it brought to the daily lives of the people living in Waxahachie. Some of the citizens regretted the passing of the older ways, while others looked forward to a brighter future. Most recognized one of the greatest changes that occurred during these years—the sewing back together of the fabric of the United States.

The Civil War had greatly tested the strength of a democratic country to overcome marked differences and persevere. Although it ended with a unified country, most southerners held firmly to the belief in their right to secede and the rightness of their cause. Through the years, these aggressive feelings subsided and became less marked and less visible. Although southerners (Waxahachie, Texas was indeed a southern city at the time) still considered themselves to be quite distinct and different from northerners, they found common ground.

Waxahachians first proved their loyalty to the United States flag when asked to volunteer for the Spanish-American War in 1898. More than 30 young men gathered at the city hall to organize a military and cavalry company on April 23, two months after the *Maine* mysteriously exploded in Havana's harbor and two days before president William McKinley asked Congress to declare war on Spain. The "glorious little war," as the Spanish-American War was called, lasted only four months and ended with the United States freeing Cuba from its colonial mother Spain. The young men from Waxahachie, who drilled every night between April and July, were finally called up for action. Additionally, a black company was formed by local African Americans who enlisted to serve and two women, Mollie Timmins and Maggie Collier, volunteered to serve as nurses in the Red Cross. The city also proudly enlisted the youngest man to volunteer in the war, Willie McClanahan, who at 13 signed up with the full consent of both parents. Though young, the boy was said to be the size of a full-grown man and acted "more manly than some with more birthdays behind them."

The Spanish-American War went a great distance in healing the wounds left from the Civil War. Like a bandage, the war wrapped the various regions and bound them together for a united cause. Patriotism soared during the war, and red, white, and blue flags and bunting hung proudly from home porches and shop windows. Americans North and South joined hands to fight for a cause they deemed just.

On November 2, 1912, the local United Daughters of the Confederacy chapter dedicated a Confederate monument to the county's fighting men. Thousands of citizens attended the ceremony where young children, dressed in their finest, sang the "Bonnie Blue Flag" and the old veterans let out a loud rebel yell.

This group photograph shows some of the men who volunteered from Waxahachie to serve in World War I. Many of the area men were shipped to France and saw heavy action in the forests around Cherbourg. Notice the African-American man in the photograph. Several black citizens from Waxahachie volunteered to serve in the war.

Roberta Green Thompson, shown here in 1918, was one of many young women who volunteered to serve in World War I as a Red Cross nurse. She later married Waxahachie native Sam Watson, who also volunteered in the war.

Similarly, when war broke out in Europe in 1914, Americans once again joined hands, overcoming their regional differences to mount a united front. Although the United States did not become officially involved in World War I until 1917, the people of Waxahachie followed the war in Europe closely—newspaper headlines daily told of the horrific deaths on Flanders's Fields, of an entire generation of young English and French men (boys, really) who had sacrificed their lives for their countries.

It was no surprise then to Waxahachie when President Woodrow Wilson asked Congress for a war resolution against Imperial Germany in April 1917. During the previous month, German submarines sank five United States merchant ships, despite the country's official neutral status, an act most Americans found intolerable. Coupled with Germany's years of aggressive actions—such as the 1915 sinking of the *Lusitania*, an English-owned passenger liner that carried nearly 1,200 people to their deaths, including 128 Americans—the people of the United States were prepared to follow Wilson into a war that promised to "make the world safe for democracy."

More than 250 men from Ellis County served in World War I and more than half received some kind of wound or war-related illness. Sixty-six men from the county paid the ultimate sacrifice, losing their lives on the fields of battle

Jo Van Marchbanks was the only man from Waxahachie to be killed during World War I. Marchbanks was wounded in September 1918, taken prisoner by the Germans, and died in a German hospital in October 1918.

in England and France, many having seen action in and around the forests of Cherbourg. Some, like Marvin E. Singleton (later president of Citizens National Bank) served their country at home, working in high-ranking governmental positions. So great was the city's contribution to the war effort, that a new United States merchant ship was christened the *S.S. Waxahachie* in May 1919.

Although the men who enlisted to serve overseas worked directly in the war effort, those left behind attempted to serve their country, too. The many women's clubs in town answered the call of the Red Cross and made hospital supplies—bandages, gowns, and sheets—for their boys. They participated in the various food drives, going without meat on Mondays and without wheat products on Tuesdays, and learned to can food and grow their own vegetables in "victory gardens." The ladies also created a recreational center in town for servicemen passing through on the train on their way to training at Camp Travis in San Antonio, providing cookies and doughnuts, cold drinks, and conversation. Additionally, the various women's clubs proudly purchased a total of $16,800 in war bonds. Although the community's ladies worked hard to help the war effort, they did not stop when the war ended. They organized and planted a memorial hedge in 1919 in honor of Waxahachie's only casualty, Jo Van F. Marchbanks.

Jo Van Marchbanks grew up in Waxahachie and was 22 years old when the United States declared war on Germany. Claiming to honor the spirit of his father, an old Confederate soldier, Marchbanks enlisted as a private in Company F, of the 359th Infantry, 90th Division, a regiment composed mainly of Ellis, Hill, and Navarro County boys. Training in San Antonio along with many of his friends, his regiment received orders in June 1918 to prepare to leave for France.

Engaging the enemy first in Rheims in part of the St. Mihiel drive and then in the Meuse-Argonne offensive, Marchbanks was wounded in September 1918 and taken prisoner by the Germans. He was immediately taken to a hospital and cared for by the enemy.

"Dear Mother," Marchbanks wrote home, "I am wounded in a German Hospital, a prisoner of war. Doing nicely. Good Treatment. Lots of Love." Marchbanks's family never received another letter from him. Though making the best of his situation, he had been badly wounded. Shot in the shoulder and chest by machine gun bullets and shoved into a shell hole by a buddy who was trying to protect him, Marchbanks was hit again when another shell exploded nearby, breaking his left cheekbone and destroying one eye. Marchbanks died from these wounds on October 25, 1918. A comrade wrote of the Waxahachie boy, "his

Waxahachie hosted a memorial parade in honor of Jo Van Marchbanks, the only man from the city to die in World War I. Remembrance ceremonies were held for the 61 other men from Ellis County who died fighting in the war.

regiment is immensely proud of one who, like him, so generously paid the last full measure of devotion for his country."

Though the loss of Marchbanks and the 61 other boys from Ellis County who died in the war was felt deeply, most of the town's citizens looked to the 1920s as a time of renewed hope and prosperity. It was a part of that desire to look ahead, not to dwell on the past, that drove Waxahachie's businessmen to try to attract Major League baseball teams to the city.

The Detroit Tigers and Ty Cobb's presence in the city in 1916 had brought excitement and anticipation to the community. Many hoped that baseball might do the same again in the years following World War I. The Cincinnati Reds spent the spring of 1919 training in Waxahachie—exciting enough, but the community watched eagerly the next October when the Reds, making it to the World Series, squared off against the Chicago White Sox. Waxahachie's baseball fans (and there were many because baseball was the city's favorite sport) were thrilled when the Reds pulled out a victory against the Sox, but they were shocked along with the rest of the nation when a few months later, they learned that the Sox had thrown the series—a fiasco quickly dubbed the "black sox scandal."

Thrown games or not, the people of Waxahachie were dedicated to their baseball. When the White Sox agreed to train in Waxahachie in the spring of 1920, fans came out, as much to see the famed scandalous team as to watch their star pitcher, Tris Speaker, throw the ball.

Waxahachie loved its baseball teams. Paul Richards starred on the Waxahachie Indians 1925 team and went on to play in the major leagues.

Although baseball remained the most popular sport in Waxahachie, basketball and football began to gain popularity. By the 1910s, the high school supported a girls' basketball team.

Though professional baseball attracted a lot of the town's attention, Waxahachians loved their own hometown high school team the most. Putting together a string of 65 consecutive victories (including two against the New York Yankees in exhibition games), the high school team received the honor of having the most consecutive wins of any baseball team, whether amateur, semi, or professional. With Paul Richards playing third base, shortstop, or pitcher, Waxahachie's team remained unbeatable throughout the 1920s. Richards went on to the big leagues, but so did 14 other boys who played on the high school team during the decade. Baseball was taken so seriously in the town that the chamber of commerce recruited players from out of state. If the coach learned that there was a farm boy in Georgia who could play ball, one of the town's businessmen went to Georgia and told his daddy that there was a job waiting for him in Waxahachie—a mixed blessing, probably, for many of the farmers—a job, but in a town most had never heard of!

Waxahachie planned to change that. The 1920s dawned brightly for the city. Though cotton prices varied widely, most planters, tenants, and sharecroppers believed that the market would eventually stabilize and return to its pre-World War I parity. Their optimism proved unfounded. Throughout the 1920s, farmers found all the agricultural markets slipping, not just cotton, and while the rest of the country seemed to be riding high—roaring even—farmers watched as they grew deeper in debt.

Perhaps it was for the best that the people of Waxahachie could not see into their futures. The Depression years proved desperate for a great many. Unemployment and starvation were evidenced on many street corners. Town folk's memories of Waxahachie's golden days, when cotton reigned king, remained fresh. Most looked back on the period between 1877 and 1929 fondly, knowing that they had experienced something wonderful and unique—the fruition of their ancestors' hard work and the expansion of their own progressive ideas and dreams. The community had grown beyond the small frontier village it had been in 1850 when it was founded and had come to represent agricultural abundance and educational excellence. Although poor farmers in Georgia might not have recognized the name Waxahachie, most Texans had heard of the town, perhaps because of the large quantity and high quality of cotton grown in the region, but more likely because the town annually hosted the Chautauqua Assembly, a two-week-long encampment that combined cultural uplift with good fun.

Waxahachie built its first city hall around 1898. Apart from handling city business, the building also housed the town's volunteer fire department, who posed with their state-of-the-art equipment.

5. A Great Moral and Educational Force

Anne Matthews opened her eyes slowly. The sun shone through the canvas at an angle, slicing a perfect crescent across her face. Raising her head from her pillow, she could already hear Cook frying bacon under the tent's canopy. She inhaled deeply and could almost taste the fried eggs and buttermilk biscuits that would accompany the meat. Leaving her gown behind, Anne dressed quickly and pulled the sheets up to make her cot. Although she lived only a few blocks away, Anne had spent the night in her neighbor's tent, camping in Chautauqua Park (though until recently it had been called West End Park).

"So sleeping beauty woke up," Cook teased, but Anne took no notice. It was the first day of the annual Chautauqua, and she had been looking forward to this moment for an entire year. "Now leave that bacon," Cook called, as Anne stole another piece from the warming plate, "there won't be none left for breakfast."

"I'm not hungry," Anne declared, running off, weaving between the tents. She was heading toward the creek, and although it was early, she could already hear the sounds of children laughing and splashing in the swimming hole that the Chautauqua leaders had made during the winter months by damming a deep section of Waxahachie Creek. There she found her best friends wading and trying to catch minnows. "Anne, come here and see this one, it sparkles," they called to her.

Looking up, Anne could see the softness of the morning sun between the boughs of the large pecan trees. Where the light touched the water, bursts of fire seemed to reflect off the limestone and fool's gold that lined the creek's bottom. Anne twirled around, taking the whole world in: the creek's gently sloping banks, the children smiling, and just beyond the rise, an entire tent city. Beautiful and white and spanning as far as she could see, the park was a wonderland of sights, sounds, and smells.

Chautauqua Park extended out over 60 acres and there seemed to be people camping out over most of the land. Many of the occupants of the more than 200 tents were already up, the women making breakfast on oil stoves or over campfires, and the men visiting and drinking coffee out of tin cups. After breakfast had been finished and the dishes washed, the adults mingled. Meeting their new neighbors (whom they would be camping near for the next two weeks),

As an adult, Anne Matthews recalled how her brothers and sisters would spend all day playing in Waxahachie Creek. The family visited the park often, not just during the Chautauqua encampment.

renewing friendships from the year's previous Chautauqua, and embracing their old friends and family.

Anne's stomach rumbled. "Meet you at Graham's Tent this afternoon," she called to her friends and, though she hated to tear herself away from the creek, she climbed up the bank and headed back to see if Cook had saved her any breakfast.

Passing between two tents, Anne watched as a cat climbed up a nearby tree. A small spotted dog yelped. Laughing, Anne called out, "Here Spotty I'll take you home." Anne gathered the little dog in her arms, still fighting to get at the cat, and made her way into the clearing that surrounded the auditorium. The large eight-sided building was quiet now, but by the evening, its seats would be filled and even its opened windows would be used as benches. Although the structure seated 2,500 people, opening night at the Chautauqua was always crowded. Locals purchased reserved seats, many closing their stores for the afternoon so that they would arrive in plenty of time. Like Anne Matthews's family, many people from Waxahachie walked or rode the mule streetcars each day the few blocks to Chautauqua Park, west of downtown and only a short stroll. Although some of the townsfolk camped out, like Anne's neighbor, most of the campers came from outside Waxahachie. People traveled from all over Texas to come to the Chautauqua, and some even came from other states. All, like Anne, loved the annual assembly.

There was much to enjoy about the Chautauqua: the smell of the park in the morning when all the families prepared breakfast, the sounds of laughter after hearing a much loved joke, the fancy tents—some people brought carpets and ice boxes—and the fellowship and friendship. Although there were many delightful things about Chautauqua, most people came to be a part of the evenings' programs.

The Chautauqua Assembly meant two weeks of educational lectures and cultural uplift. It promised famed professors, admired politicians, renowned musicians, and highbrow opera. A mixture of educational programming and down-home entertainment, Chautauqua had a little something for everyone.

In 1874, Methodist preacher John H. Vincent and Ohio businessman Lewis Miller instituted a summer school program for Sunday school teachers along the shores of Chautauqua Lake in western New York. The summer camp prepared the participants to teach Bible classes and trained them in how to organize and manage Sunday school. The program received such high praise that the assembly grew larger and larger each successive year until, within ten years, more than 150,000 people traveled to Chautauqua to take part in the summer-long sessions. No longer a camp, the assembly occupied 225 acres and housed and educated the visitors in 1,200 buildings, which included an open-air auditorium, hotel, restaurants, classrooms, and private residences.

Knowing that there were thousands of Americans who would have liked to take part in the summer Chautauqua Assemblies in New York, but simply could not, Vincent established the Chautauqua Literary and Scientific Circle (CLSC) as a means of promoting general intelligence, education, and culture among the people. Begun in 1878, the program entailed a complete "study at home" course. The students who enrolled received all their materials and support from the

Built in 1902, the 8-sided Chautauqua Pavilion seated more than 2,500 people. Still in use today, the structure was built entirely of wood in less than two months.

CLSC, which distributed a detailed course syllabus to follow. Participants devoted one hour each day to their studies and at the end of each year, took a written test. If they passed, they went on to the next year's materials. At the end of four years, the students completed the course materials and received a diploma declaring their graduation from the CLSC. The basic course consisted mainly of classical literature, but separate certificates might be earned by studying the special courses of art, language, science, or music. To round out the program, Vincent suggested that students attempt to participate in a summer camp; several were springing up across the United States by the 1880s, because the encampments combined educational uplift with recreation and entertainment in a wholesome and moral environment.

Waxahachie's first association with Chautauqua came in 1889 when a group of young ladies got together and formed the Sappho Chautauqua Literary and Scientific Circle. The young unmarried women believed that their educational opportunities were limited and began the club as a means of improving themselves through systematic reading. In other words, they hoped to give themselves a "college outlook" when college educations were still primarily limited to men. Willia Getzendaner, daughter of one of the town's leading and most wealthy citizens, served as the organization's president. She and the other dozen women who joined Sappho (named in honor of the only major female writer whose works

A DINNER OF DOVES.

The "Doves," a ladies organization, hosted dinner on the Chautauqua grounds during the 1902 encampment. "Doves" from all over the state gathered and enjoyed the fellowship.

At an early Chautauqua assembly, campers posed for a photograph in front of their tents. People came from throughout Texas and even farther away to participate in the Chautauqua; many of them camped out for the two-week period.

survived from classical Greece and Rome) met weekly to discuss their readings. They set out to finish the course in only three years instead of the suggested four and, although a few of the women did not complete the program, most did and received their Chautauqua diplomas. *The Chautauquan*, the institute's monthly journal, helped the club's members stay on schedule over the years. Filled with assignments, news items, and instructions, the journal was the most popular monthly publication in the country for a time.

Ten years later, when the people of Waxahachie were first approached with the suggestion of holding a summer Chautauqua camp, most of the townspeople were already familiar with the Chautauqua Assembly in New York (some wealthier citizens had visited the main assembly) and the individual study course that had been created in association with it (some had watched their daughters undertake the reading course, while others had pursued the home-study themselves). Over the years, Waxahachie had consistently supported adult education in the form of visiting lecturers and exhibits, so it was not surprising that many of the town's leaders were excited about bringing Chautauqua to the community.

CHURCH HELPER HEADQUARTERS.

Many of Waxahachie's organizations erected tents during the Chautauqua to provide services to visitors. The Church Helpers Headquarters introduced visitors to other campers who shared their denomination.

Having met in Glen Rose, about 75 miles west of Waxahachie, the summer encampment sponsored by the Texas Synod of the Cumberland Presbyterian Church announced that it would immediately begin looking for a new city in which to hold its Chautauqua assembly. Glen Rose was too inaccessible, the Synod argued, and the local people were disinterested in the summer camp and had not tried to promote it in any way. Unlike their neighbors, Waxahachians were enthusiastic about the venture from the start. Reverend J.C. Smith, pastor of the local Cumberland Presbyterian Church, led the effort in attracting the assembly to Waxahachie. Organizing a committee, Smith agreed to take a summer sabbatical and attend the assembly in New York to see the "mother" program first hand. Another citizen, T.A. Ferris, a banker, attended the Texas-Colorado Chautauqua Assembly in Boulder, Colorado (begun by Texas teachers looking for a closer site than New York to create a permanent summer assembly, but a location that still offered a vacation-like atmosphere) to study the effects on a community that hosted a summer encampment.

Waxahachie's Chautauqua committee reconvened and all agreed that the town should bid for the annual assembly. Area churches joined together, regardless of denomination, and supported the decision along with the town's businessmen, who saw the potential commercial opportunities in having hundreds, maybe even thousands, of people visiting the city each summer. The town offered the Synod at least 20 acres along Waxahachie Creek—land dotted with pecan trees—in the city's suburbs. They promised that the land was easily reached; two major railroads had terminals within 200 yards and a streetcar ran directly to the park. In addition to the trees and beautiful creek, the park had an artesian water source. The Chautauqua committee also agreed to gravel the walkways, build drives, and hang electric lights throughout the park. The town's newspaper relayed the committee's sentiments when it declared, "of course Waxahachie wants the Chautauqua. The town that has too many enterprises cannot be found on a map of Texas, and when we are offered a new enterprise it is our duty to take it."

The Texas Synod of the Cumberland Presbyterian Church enthusiastically chose Waxahachie as the meeting site for its 1900 Chautauqua assembly, as excited about the assembly's potential as was the town. The decision to relocate to Waxahachie linked the community with 292 other United States towns that would host similar gatherings over the years. Eventually, 31 states hosted Chautauqua camps—all independent of the "mother" in New York, but based on the same premise: a vacation atmosphere enlivened by educational lectures, music, and cultural programming within a morally upright environment.

Fulfilling its promise, Waxahachie's Chautauqua assembly immediately began to prepare for the first encampment. Men strung electric lights in the trees,

There were often more than 200 tents erected in Chautauqua Park for the annual encampment. Texans enjoyed camping out, and many erected elaborate tents with fans, carpets, and refrigerators.

cleared an area for tents, and built graveled sidewalks and drives. They fenced the circumference of West End Park (now Getzendaner Park) to define the encampment and to provide a hitching rail for the horse-pulled wagons. Finally, they built an open-air pavilion that seated 1,200 people.

During the last week of July and the first week of August 1900, campers inhabited more than 75 tents in West End Park. Local townspeople came out to hear the lectures, but visitors also came from all over Texas. For example, attendees traveled from Whitesboro, Jefferson, Italy, San Antonio, and Mexia, Texas and from parts of Oklahoma.

A little city seemed to have sprung up overnight. Tents surrounded the pavilion, and there was also a restaurant, barbershop, telephone booth, post office, newsstand, and a cold drink establishment on site. In case of theft, the town hired a night watchman to secure the area.

Fellowship and friendship permeated the gathering. Bible study filled morning sessions, but the attendees most enjoyed the evening programs. Lectures formed the backbone of the meetings. Local citizen Judge O.E. Dunlap, president of Citizens National Bank, illustrated a talk about his world travels with slides and carried the people from New York to Land's End, London to Gibraltar, Rome to Vesuvius, Naples to Cairo, Paris on to Scotland. Dunlap received a warm round

Each summer, a tent city sprang up in Chautauqua Park (now Getzendaner Park). Campers enjoyed the shade of the pecan trees, the meandering creek, and the fellowship that the Chautauqua assembly brought to the small town.

of applause, his speech reminiscent of Mark Twain's recently published guide to world travel, *The Innocents Abroad*.

Even more popular than Dunlap's presentation was Professor S.L. Hornbeak's chemistry demonstrations. Speaking on "the air we breathe," Hornbeak broke down the chemicals in the air and explained what could be done with the separate ingredients. He then amazed the audience with "startling" experiments.

A fortnight later, Waxahachie's Chautauqua Committee announced that the encampment had been a "good influence" and, though it required a great deal of work on the part of the board members and local citizens, the meeting had been a wonderful success. Despite the thunderstorms that hit the city on successive nights causing many of the secured lecturers to cancel, the "best" people had still come out and packed the pavilion.

With their first successful year behind them, the committee began planning the 1901 Chautauqua. Once again, West End Park filled with campers eagerly anticipating a two-week vacation where they might rest and relax and expand their educational horizons. Committee members had planned a wide range of activities and topics, which began on opening night with local judge S.P. Skinner, who spoke on "The Duties and Privileges of the New Century."

Skinner explained that "an old century has just passed; a new one is just upon us. We stand . . . on the common border of two ages; on this side we behold the past with its lessons of wisdom and experience, while over here is the veiled future, with its rich promises and immeasurable possibilities." He marveled at the new inventions that had made the world smaller, making travel possible to far away lands and, by telephones and telegraphs, the whole universe accessible in minutes. Skinner argued that these inventions made the new century one of comfort and convenience. "The busy hum of industry with its incidents of thrift and comfort will be seen and heard in every city," Skinner claimed, and Texas would lead the way.

Skinner's lecture began the 1901 encampment and each day following was given over to a special topic. One day for education and another for missions—that day organized solely by the women who planned the day's programs and presented all the lectures. By far, though, the most popular day of the encampment was Old Soldiers' Day, a commemoration of the city's Confederate veterans. General John B. Gordon, a brigadier general in the Confederate Army who distinguished himself at Chancellorsville, Gettysburg, and Appomatox, was the featured speaker that night and an estimated 4,000 people came out to listen attentively for more than two hours as he recounted war stories of the boys in gray. A rousing chorus of "Dixie" rounded off the evening and the rebel yell was heard far into the night around the tents.

Although the focus of the Chautauqua remained educational, recreational pursuits were never far behind. In 1901, the committee members erected swings and a croquet court for the children, and marked off a baseball field for the boys. While the younger set played games or waded in the creek, the adults visited, read, and generally relaxed. One individual commented, "what a time we have had

Attendance had grown so large that promoters built a new pavilion for the 1902 encampment. The photograph shows the eight-sided structure's interior, decorated for the evening's performance.

under the greatest trees that ever grew in Texas. Like angels of mercy these trees have shaded us, fanned us and spread their great arms above us and pronounced heaven's blessings upon us by day and night."

The 1901 Chautauqua surpassed the first year's encampment in success and attendance. Even before the two weeks were over, many of the attendees began to discuss the 1902 camp and determined that the pavilion built the year before simply would not prove adequate the following year. On August 9, 1901, interested citizens gathered at city hall and formed the Waxahachie Chautauqua Park Association and decided to build an octagonal auditorium, modeled after the eight-sided open-air auditorium at Chautauqua, New York.

After raising more than $1,600 and securing three deeds to additional land (increasing the park's size to 55 acres), the park association hired E.S. Boze, a local contractor, to head up the project. Beginning in June 1902 and finishing less than two months later, before the year's encampment the last week of July, Boze built the structure entirely of wood at a cost of $2,750. The building had large wooden windows that lifted into the walls to create an open-air pavilion. Inset into the south side, the wooden stage projected out into the seating area, and dressing rooms were stationed behind and underneath the stage. A painted canvas curtain could be drawn across the performance area, electric lights illuminated the building, and the entire floor was planked. Boze had the building ready for the opening night of the 1902 camp and an estimated 5,000 individuals enjoyed the new building.

Chautauqua Park, as it was being called by 1902, filled with tents; the newspaper reported that 175 tents had already been set in place, 12 more had been ordered, and the park association estimated that at least 200 would eventually be requested. The old pavilion had been turned into a dining hall and hundreds enjoyed their mid-day meals under its roof at a nominal cost. Dr. Andrews, Chancellor of the University of Nebraska and a Union veteran, spoke one night on the "Character of Robert E. Lee." The newspaper reported that he was the first Union soldier to speak to the people of Waxahachie about the Confederacy. Although the audience was respectful of his lecture, they enjoyed the quartet that followed him more. The male quartette proved the favorite musical group during the encampment. The singers, four of Waxahachie's leading businessmen who sang regularly and even toured to other Chautauqua camps, included Mr. Coleman, a lawyer and real estate agent who was 6 feet, 6 inches tall; T.H. Wear, the heavyweight of the group who managed the new Century Store; A.D. Thompson, who was connected with the Waxahachie Loan and Trust and had a "splendidly trained bass voice"; and the featherweight W.S. Newton, who sang the leading parts.

HASH HOUSE.

The Hashhouse was one of many tents erected during the 1902 Chautauqua. In addition to renting tents, the encampment's promoters also strung tiny white lights throughout the trees to light the park during the evening hours.

The program cover for the 1904 Chautauqua assembly promised a full session. Chemistry demonstrations and lectures about Shakespeare's life and works were popular during the early years of the encampment.

The Graham Bachelor's Tent was erected throughout the 1910s and offered the young people who attended Chautauqua a private place to socialize.

With the new auditorium in place, Waxahachie's Chautauqua assembly was ready for expansion and each successive year, the encampment attracted more attention. Throughout the 1900s, the attendance continued to grow. The ideal programs combined lectures with music, variety shows, or drama, but always within a framework of spiritual and cultural activities.

Throughout the United States, Chautauqua assemblies popularized education and were the primary means of diffusing knowledge during the early part of the twentieth century. Beyond their educational value, the camps were truly American in nature. Clinging to the idea of their Puritan work ethic, Americans generally rejected leisure as being European and aristocratic. Chautauqua encampments meshed these conflicting values, allowing people to take vacations and still consider themselves industrious by creating the first working vacations!

Although twenty-first-century Americans might not consider listening to lectures work, many of the people who attended Waxahachie's Chautauqua believed that they were working to enlarge their general intellectual outlook. Throughout the 1900s, the camps remained focused on daily studies and nightly lectures, enlivened by entertainment. Discussions and demonstrations in the sciences, especially chemistry, remained popular, as did readings and interpretations of Shakespeare's works and life and times. Soldiers spoke about their experiences in the recent Spanish-American War (1898) and naval officers thrilled crowds by discussing their heroic encounter with the enemy in the subsequent war in the Philippines (1900–1904).

The encampments did not consist entirely of work and plenty of attention was paid to the social side of Chautauqua. The children found entertainment in the creek—the boys diving from the high limbs of the trees that towered over the dammed swimming area—in organized games, and in the general strength of their imaginations.

The young people were well provided for, too. In 1903, a group of the town's young men and eligible bachelors formed a little group that they called the Graham Bachelor's Club and erected a tent that they continued to put up throughout the 1900s where the young men and ladies could gather and visit. The tent was enormous—one report claimed that it was as large as a circus tent—and had scalloped flaps, rugs on the floors, tables for whist and dominoes, and a water cooler to quench the ladies' thirst. During the day, the tent was often empty, but after the evening programs, it overflowed with games of Forty-two played around with much flirtation.

Waxahachie sponsored one of the oldest and most attended Chautauqua encampments in Texas (at least six other towns unsuccessfully attempted similar camps), but found itself in trouble by the 1910s. Although the camps remained popular, independent sites like Waxahachie found that they could no longer attract popular lectures and entertainers. The world of Chautauqua had been commercialized and to keep up, the city had to join one of the circuits recently established.

Keith Vawter organized the first Chautauqua circuit, hoping to find a way to ensure the availability of talent while decreasing the miles that speakers and entertainers traveled. During the 1910s, there were a handful of well-known and much sought-after speakers, musicians, singers, and ventriloquists that all the Chautauquas wanted to hire (presidential candidate William Jennings Bryan was the most popular Chautauqua lecturer), but how to coordinate all those dates and defray the expenses and wear and tear of travel? Vawter believed that if he could group the independent camps into a circuit, then they could all hire the same entertainers and their general expenses would be reduced.

Vawter ran the Redpath Chautauqua Circuit with talent working on a rotation basis in sequence. Vawter assigned a day to each entertainer and they always performed on that day, no matter what town they were in. The predictability lowered costs in general and provided for better entertainment. In 1912, Waxahachie joined the Redpath-Horner Circuit and gained access to national entertainers, greatly increasing the appeal of the Chautauqua and once again increasing the attendance.

To advertise the change in talent, Waxahachie's Ad Club, Commercial Club, and Retail Merchant Association organized three "trade trips." Thirty-three cars decked with banners advertising the Chautauqua assembled on the west side of Waxahachie's square on June 7. Leaving around 1:00 in the afternoon, more than 150 people piled into the cars; the first few contained a band and a motorcycle led up the rear. The parade wound through part of the county, stopping to let individuals make speeches and for the band to play to assembled crowds. The caravan traveled for five hours, advertising the encampment, and the group made three subsequent trips to other areas in the county.

The change in venue and advertising push worked—the 1912 Chautauqua was one of Waxahachie's largest and best. A season ticket, good for the entire two weeks, cost $2 for adults and $1 for children ages eight to fourteen. Each evening's entertainment was priced differently, based on the talent's popularity, and ranged between 25¢ for a single performance to free. The eighth day, designated Waxahachie Day, attracted the largest crowds. Local businesses closed for the afternoon, the city almost buzzing with anticipation.

By early evening, Chautauqua Park was filling to capacity. Horses were hitched to the fence around the park, swatting flies with their tails and eating the hay their owners had left for them. The campers lingered around their tents, the men waiting for their wives to finish dressing, laughing amongst themselves at the lengths the women folk went to for the sake of fashion.

The mule streetcars made regular trips from downtown and from the train terminals. Women and children crowded into the seats on the cars and the men stood, some even hanging out the open doors in the front and back. Thousands converged on the park, eagerly awaiting the evening's performance.

By dusk, the auditorium was filled, seemingly bursting over with people. Laughing and joking, the local farmers and their families had filled the back rows—the front seats were reserved for season ticket holders, which were usually purchased by campers and city folk. Many had brought blankets to make pallets

HAVE SOME DINNER WITH US?

A promotional photograph taken in 1902, the campers encouraged other Texans to come have "dinner with us." Such advertising worked: each year Waxahachie's Chautauqua attendance grew. At times, more than 5,000 people gathered to hear lectures and music.

in the aisles for their little ones, kept entertained over the next few hours with crackers and jugs of water. Although the benches were filled, more people wanted to see and hear the program than there were seats, and they leaned in the large windows that had been raised into the ceiling while some simply stood around the auditorium hoping to catch a glimpse.

In the dressing room, two opera singers prepared themselves for the show, the circuit manager having excitedly told them that they would perform to a sold out crowd. The singers, while having performed with the Metropolitan Grand Opera, were delighted, and they thrilled the crowd with their majestic voices and earnest interpretations. After several encores, the singers finally retired only to be followed by a South Sea Islander who acted out his native dramas in full costume.

After the performance, the sleepy children were gathered and the farm families piled back into their wagons, the ride home shortened by talk of the night's show. Over the camp, the stars glistened high in the summer sky and tiny white lights threaded through the trees mimicked the night sky. The tenters returned to their campsites, many gathering at individual fires to relive the performance. Their children's eyes were blurry with sleep, but the adults, wide awake with excitement, talked late into the night.

That night's performance remained a topic of conversation for the following year; Chautauqua seemed to hold that kind of magic for the people who gathered

ICE WATER FOR ALL.

Ice water was made freely available to all campers at Chautauqua. Several tents encouraged campers to "come inside" and enjoy the crystal clear and cold water available.

to see it. They listened to music from Italy and saw a native from the South Sea Islands, all from the comfort of their own neighborhood. While the encampment lasted only two weeks, during that brief period, the attendees might be exposed to the whole world and that was essentially the greatest value of the summer camps. A largely rural people could travel across Europe, discuss the most pressing political questions, and be introduced to amazing advances in science. Chautauqua kept the American people abreast of the changes in the world while reminding them of humanity's varied and interesting past and future.

While much stayed the same when Waxahachie's camp went from an independent organization to part of a larger circuit in 1912, a few things did change. Lectures ceased to be the backbone of the programs; Americans began demanding more entertainment and less education, and while many of the encampments still retained an element of intellectual pursuit, most simply catered to those demanding recreation. Talent became more exclusive, and Waxahachie competed with towns throughout the Midwest and Southwest to ensure that they could book big name performers.

Several nationally famous groups performed in Waxahachie during the 1910s. One of the most popular was Bohumir Kryl's Bohemian Band. Kryl was a protégé of John Phillip Sousa and thrilled his audiences with a rendition of the "Anvil Chorus" (*Il Trovatore*). Kryl used four large anvils during the musical, clanged by men in leather aprons with hammers, while an electrical device sent sparks flying across the darkened stage.

Perhaps not as popular but still widely anticipated were The Morphets: Masters of Magic, Melody, and Mirth. The Morphets illuminated the stage without the house lights by holding a three-burner chandelier fitted with a Welsbach gas mantle. An assistant held the chandelier while Morphet placed the end of a rubber tube to his mouth, breathed deeply, and, while blowing his breath out, lit the mantle with a match, casting a brilliant light across the auditorium. The lead was a magician and illusionist, and his associates added to the entertainment by providing acts of ventriloquism.

Although most of the talent during the second decade of Chautauqua came from national and international bookings, Waxahachie still provided a few of its own entertainers. Dr. A.E. Turner, a professor at Trinity University, lectured on the "Eternal City," with stereo-opticon views of the Roman Coliseum. His talk dealt with the many tragedies that had befallen Rome, a lecture that Turner went on to present at Chautauqua encampments across the nation.

Although entertainment had edged out lecturing by the 1910s (Swiss bell ringers, orchestras, glee clubs, string quartets, and bands competed with grand opera stars and Bavarian folk singers for most popular performers), Chautauqua still maintained room for educational and social instruction. Americans favored lectures on religion, temperance, and politics, and many politicians found that they could gain widespread recognition, and thus increase their voter appeal, by working the Chautauqua circuit. While William Jennings Bryan, four-time presidential candidate, remained the most popular speaker—he once gave

50 lectures in 28 days—other politicians like Warren G. Harding found that campaigning on the circuit could pay off in big ways. Harding was elected president in 1920.

Most of the political talk centered on progressive thought, and reformers found ready audiences throughout the United States. Talk of railroad and tariff reform and the taxation of the rich undermined an essentially conservative electorate and introduced radical ideas—some teetering on socialism—to the backbone of the United States.

Lest the children be forgotten in all the seriousness, the Redpath-Horner circuit organized Junior Chautauquas. The "junior" girl, hired to entertain the little ones, told them stories, organized games and parties, performed stunts, and supervised athletic contests. Oftentimes, the children formed "junior" towns, taking turns serving as mayor, police chief, and town clerk. The children most enjoyed the pageant they performed at the end of Chautauqua for their parents. The programs usually dealt with patriotism, children's health issues, or local government—dramatizing for their parents the need for playgrounds and sports fields, and essentially repeating progressive themes similar to their parent's discussions.

Throughout the 1910s, Chautauqua remained popular, although primarily in rural areas. Cities, with all their permanent entertainment options (opera houses, vaudeville shows, and the new silent movies playing) could never muster the crowds that overwhelmed camps in places like Waxahachie. But by the 1920s, Chautauquas throughout the country faced dramatic declines as travel became more accessible and Americans had a wider range of choices when it came to recreation and education.

Chautauqua's 50th anniversary year, 1924, marked the movement's highpoint. Banners flew in 12,000 towns that summer and an estimated 30 million Americans—one-third of the entire population—saw Chautauqua programs. Attendance began to decline immediately after 1924, steadily and rapidly. Not only had automobile ownership proliferated, allowing rural Americans to visit cities whenever they chose, but hundreds of thousands of Americans had purchased radios and could hear music, lectures, and dramas in their own homes whenever they wanted with just the turn of a knob.

Waxahachie continued its Chautauqua program throughout the 1920s, but like encampments elsewhere in the United States, the city's summer camp declined rapidly. The city's last large-scale effort to attract audiences to its Chautauqua auditorium occurred in 1927 when Will Rogers, the famous humorist, agreed to stop over in the city and perform.

Rogers arrived by train on a Saturday afternoon and was scheduled to perform at 8:30 that night. Local newspapers ran ads throughout the previous week advertising Rogers's performance: articles, photos, descriptions of the humorist's life, career, and character filled a page each day.

The city had placed speakers in various trees around the auditorium and amplified radio music throughout the park. Expecting a large turn-out (Rogers usually played to sold-out audiences), the evening's organizers were disappointed

The increased usage of personal automobiles severely decreased the number of passengers using the interurban. By 1948, the electric passenger train discontinued service, ending 60 years of quality public transportation in Waxahachie.

that only a few dozen people came to hear one of the most well known men in the country. Rogers went on stage as if the auditorium was packed and spoke for 101 minutes. He related his last trip to Europe and cracked jokes about Mussolini. He discussed United States foreign policy, the League of Nations, and disarmament (all controversial topics in the post–World War I years) and told stories about Texas's former governor Jim Ferguson.

Some locals attributed the low turn-out to poor advertising; others saw it as part of the larger trend away from such performances. On the eve of the Great Depression, Chautauqua and other similar programs had rapidly declined in popularity, and the lean years ahead spelled their extinction.

Although Waxahachie continued to host a Chautauqua program for another three years (through 1930), Rogers's program marked the passing of an era. At its peak, there were 21 different companies operating 93 separate circuits throughout the United States and Canada. Historians estimate that more than 8,580 towns hosted some kind of Chautauqua camp and presented programs to almost 36 million people.

The camps provided many benefits to the individuals who attended them. In addition to their social nature, the lectures kept Americans abreast of current political and social issues. Called the "one free platform in America," Chautauqua provided a relatively unbiased place of discussion for national and world affairs. Millions of Americans learned of slum clearance, woman suffrage, the eight-hour workday, pure food and drug legislation, city planning, and world disarmament. The lectures introduced the people to innovation and reform and attempted to "uplift" them—encouraging them to live cheerfully as neighbors and as citizens of their communities.

Chautauqua officials built bridges over several bends of Chautauqua Park. Campers were then able to erect tents on both sides of Waxahachie Creek and easily reach the main pavilion.

In addition to the personal benefits derived from the summer programs, the communities that sponsored Chautauqua found that the camps changed the nature of their towns. Important national figures visited the rural cities, and many had dinner in the homes of local leading citizens—connecting city leaders and national leaders in ways previously impossible. Such meetings helped these local leaders develop new strategies for working together as communities. A spirit of boosterism permeated many of the rural cities as the citizens came together and cleaned up their towns to prepare for visitors.

The people of Waxahachie benefited in many ways from the yearly Chautauqua. The Texas town had connected itself with the rest of world while encouraging the world to visit the town. The general intellectual stimulation proved invigorating—though the programs remained rigidly segregated, and Waxahachie's African-American population did not enjoy the many benefits Chautauqua brought to the community.

Despite the advantages the summer camps offered, they had virtually disappeared by the early 1930s. Waxahachie's Chautauqua experienced declining attendances throughout the 1920s and formally ceased to exist in 1930. The camping grounds, long known as Chautauqua Park, soon became called Getzendaner Park for William H. Getzendaner, local banker and planter, who had assumed the land's note and donated the property to the city in 1914.

Over the next 40 years, Waxahachie's citizens enjoyed the shade of the large trees in the park and the creek that wound through the old pecans. Couples brought picnics to the grounds and citywide barbecues were held along the creek banks. Ladies quilted in the afternoons in the open-air pavilion, while their children pretended to be knights in shining armor rescuing fair maidens and cowboys chasing wild Indians.

Over the years, the grounds were changed and improved. Civic leaders piped water to the park and built a wading pool on the west end. A baseball field was marked off and children spent Saturday afternoons playing on the diamond. The auditorium continued to host the city's functions—visiting politicians stood on the same stage where the yearly beauty queen was chosen. The local schools used the octagonal structure for plays, recitals, and graduation, and several generations of Waxahachians grew up visiting the park and attending programs in the auditorium.

By the late 1960s, the Chautauqua auditorium (built in 1902) had fallen into disrepair. City manager Jack Whitt requested that the building be boarded up to prevent children from entering and possibly injuring themselves in the "rickety, termite-ridden building" in 1971. The city consulted an engineering firm regarding the structure, and the engineers determined that the property was beyond repair because of termite destruction and needed to be demolished.

While most of Waxahachie's citizens showed little interest in the old building, a few took steps to try to save the structure. Acting city manager David Leslie consulted a local pest control company owned by Don Stroope, a native of Waxahachie, and he determined (after a careful examination of the structure's undercarriage) that the termite damage was negligible because the old building had been constructed from the heartwood of the longleaf southern pine, a wood so dense and so saturated with resin that termites cannot digest it.

Armed with this new information, Josephine Ruskin, Ford Lane, and Forest and Ola Upshaw pleaded with the council to reconsider. While small in number, the group worked hard on behalf of the building. Applying with the state of Texas, the group received a Texas State Historical Marker in 1971 for the old structure and listed the building on the National Register of Historical Places in 1974.

Leading an effort to restore the auditorium, Josephine and Robert Ruskin worked vigilantly to raise the funds necessary to repair and improve the building. Within a year, the restoration was complete. The city formally reopened the auditorium on July 4, 1975 and Dr. Ernest Connally of the United States Department of the Interior spoke, claiming that the building represented a "link between generations bearing a message in three-dimensional tangible form of human aspiration and endeavor." Two months later, Will Rogers Jr. visited the auditorium. He spoke on "My Father's Humor" and related the career of Will Rogers Sr. He said that his father talked about the "Waxahachie crowd" of 1927 and understood him to mean a "warm and friendly audience."

Today, multiple generations visit the old auditorium. Great grandparents fondly recall the old summer encampments for the young. They sit together on the same wooden benches where scores of people sat before them, rural people who traveled to Rome and Paris by the only means available to them—the Chautauqua Assembly.

Once again, Waxahachie hosts an annual Chautauqua. In 1999, Kirk Hunter and Maureen Moore attended the "mother" Chautauqua, which had managed to survive while virtually all the other encampments disassembled, and joined the Chautauqua Network, a group of individual organizations that continue to hold assemblies.

After coming back home, the two took the reigns of the Chautauqua Preservation Society (first created to raise funds to restore the auditorium) and organized the first Chautauqua Assembly in Waxahachie in almost 70 years. Although the assembly meets for only one day, the program, held yearly in September, is packed and reflects the general diversity of the early assemblies with a mixture of lectures and entertaining music.

Dead for many years, Chautauqua has bloomed once more in Waxahachie. While Americans in the 1930s may have found their radios, automobiles, and the easy access to entertainment that cities provided more appealing than the old assemblies, many people are now harkening back to the old pleasures of spending an evening listening to a well-known figure speak about a pressing current affair, followed by a rousing hour's worth of southern bluegrass music. Emptying out of the historical auditorium, crowds are once again strolling around the old campgrounds listening to the sounds of the night: the cricket's chirp as the firefly's luminescence tracks the eye to the stars of Texas's summer sky.

The children who attended Chautauqua in Waxahachie loved to play in the creek. By 1904, a section of the creek near the camp sites had been dammed to accommodate the growing crowds.

6. Helping the Community, Serving the Nation

Brave Bessie looked out over the wing of her plane. From her vantage point high in the sky, she could see the countless farms and miles of cotton fields that bellied up to Waxahachie, lately billing itself the queen city of the cotton belt and Coleman's hometown.

Bessie Coleman, the world's first licensed African-American pilot (male or female), grew up in Waxahachie. The 12th of 13 children, her father left the family when she was still a young girl. To ease the family's financial obligations, she went to work picking cotton and helping her mother wash and iron "white folks' " clothes. Graduating from Oak Lawn Academy, she enrolled at the Colored Agricultural and Normal University (now Langston University) in Langston, Oklahoma, but had to quit after one semester because of a lack of money. Moving to Chicago to be near a brother, Coleman worked in a series of jobs until 1920 when, acting on a lifelong dream of learning to fly and discovering that no American school would accept an African American, she traveled abroad to attend aviation school in Le Crotoy, France. After studying for ten months, she received a license in 1921, giving her the distinction of being the first African American in the world to become a licensed pilot.

Coleman returned to the United States and began flying exhibition flights all over the country, many in her native south. Her daredevil stunts and hair-raising maneuvers earned her the nickname "Brave Bessie," and she often gave lectures to schools and churches, encouraging African Americans to enter aviation.

Coleman had agreed to host an exhibition in Waxahachie, and it was one of the few times she had been back to the town where she had spent her youth. Looking out over the cotton fields, she could see one of the shanties where she had lived with her mother, brothers, and sisters. Seemingly falling apart when she was a child, the one-room shack was leaning heavily to the north, a result, Coleman knew, of the almost constant southern winds that blew across the prairie land.

"Not much has changed," she thought, as she circled the old Curtiss JN-4D plane, a World War I surplus, and began to warm up for the afternoon's exhibition. "At least this time," she told herself, "I have guaranteed that my friends and family will watch my flight alongside the whites in town."

Coleman had enthusiastically agreed to put on a heart-stopping show for Waxahachie's citizens, taking off and landing on the white school's grounds, but only if blacks were permitted to use the same entrance as whites. The town's boosters agreed to the demand and Coleman watched with great optimism as whites and blacks entered the field together, each paying the same collector for their tickets.

Coming across the field for her first aerial maneuver, Coleman was shocked and dismayed to find that once the blacks had entered the grounds, they had been sectioned off into a specific area, essentially roped into segregation. "No," she thought, "not much has changed."

In many ways, Bessie Coleman was right. Much about Waxahachie had remained the same, but the next few years would bring tremendous changes to the county seat, changes that would forever alter the demographic, social, and economic layout of the land. The Great Depression spelled disaster for the country's farmers, and few suffered worse than did the men and women of Waxahachie. Ten years later, the very nature of agriculture in the county would be forever altered—ceasing to rely solely on cotton and once again exploring its pioneering roots of diversification. As if poverty and unemployment had not rocked the city to its core, World War II spelled greater sacrifice. In terms of men and women, Ellis County bore a heavy burden offering up its youth for the greatest sacrifice, but even on the homefront, Waxahachians committed themselves to an "all out fight to the finish."

One of the many programs at Oak Lawn, in this case a sewing class, hoped to train young African-American women for the work force.

African Americans made up the largest minority group in Waxahachie in the 1930s, and most of them worked as tenant and sharecrop farmers. These families paused for a photograph before they began to hoe the fields. Both African-American men and women worked in the fields, a necessity to survive.

When Bessie Coleman flew over the Waxahachie landscape, the county led all others in Texas in terms of agricultural output: averaging at least 90,000 bales of cotton per year, but also producing sizeable corn, oat, wheat, and hay crops. Almost 54,000 people resided in Ellis County and African Americans made up the largest minority group—almost 25 percent of the entire population. Although cotton production had slipped in the late 1920s, the overwhelmingly agrarian population (more than 50 percent of the population classed themselves as farmers and, among the black families, the percentages ran to more than 80 percent) still produced more cotton than any other region in the United States.

Despite the accolades, the late 1920s proved a period of hardship for local farmers. Boll weevil, bollworm, and root rot infested the cotton crops year after year. As difficult as these problems appeared, the land suffered even more from soil erosion. Farmers, not practicing sustainable agriculture, had used up the soil, a resource once imagined unlimited that now seemed to be reaching its limit.

Perceptive businessmen in the county already knew that difficult times lay ahead, but few realized just how lean the future would prove. Most were not prepared for the news they received when they awoke on Tuesday, October 29, 1929, the most devastating single day in stock market history to that point. Black Tuesday, as it was soon called, ushered in a general economic collapse. Already

Waxahachie's business district continued to attract shoppers during the Great Depression. Many citizens gathered on the square on Saturday nights to walk, talk, and generally be seen by friends and family.

experiencing swinging agricultural prices and massive overproduction, Ellis County's farmers faced total loss—local banks began foreclosure proceedings, and tenants were left abandoned: no home (as meager as the shacks looked, they were shelter), no land, and nowhere to turn.

From the fall of 1929 to March 1932, Americans watched as Herbert Hoover sank into a malaise as deep as the Depression that gripped the nation. Although Hoover tried to combat the crisis, the country slipped into despair, hoping that the next presidential election might bring forth a leader.

Among strains of "Happy Days Are Here Again," Franklin Delano Roosevelt accepted the Democratic nomination for the presidency and easily beat Hoover in the election. Waxahachians voted overwhelmingly for Roosevelt—as much a factor of their confidence in the man as their commitment to vote a straight Democratic ticket. Roosevelt promised a new deal for the American people, and Waxahachie's citizens waited for him to deliver.

Prior to FDR, families were expected to take care of their own and if for some reason they could not, people looked to local churches for help. Society discouraged relief to the poor and destitute—part of the "survival of the fittest" mentality that pervaded the United States throughout the first part of the twentieth century—and no help could be found beyond the county level. Some local governments had attempted to aid familes and churches by creating county poor farms. Ellis County had started a poor farm in the early 1880s and while it still existed in 1932, it was filled to capacity and could not keep up with the demand for occupants.

Looking to ease the burden generally, Waxahachie's city council took unprecedented steps in creating a County Board of Relief, but it too was quickly overwhelmed. Attempting to distribute food and clothing, the board funded its operations strictly by volunteer contributions, asking families with jobs to pledge 10¢ or 25¢ a week to help local people make it through the winters.

Additionally, the council organized a campaign called, "What can you do to help your town?" Hoping to rally community spirits, the local branch of the Red Cross handed out flour for bread and clothing materials in the post office, mainly to women and their children. The city's churches collected men's shoes, clothing, quilts, and blankets and distributed them as they could. The business community encouraged people to buy locally in a campaign they called "Buy Waxahachie," and the city sponsored an unemployment drive called "Renovize Waxahachie." Chamber of commerce representatives went door-to-door asking if citizens had any work that needed to be done around their homes, regardless of the project's size. These jobs were then posted on a bulletin board downtown, "to maintain fairness," because the work was to remain open to all men and women—regardless of race.

Although these efforts proved modest compared with need, many destitute people resisted any help for as long as they could. At the time, direct relief efforts—sometimes referred to as the dole—stigmatized a person, somehow

Despite the Depression, Waxahachie's commercial district remained busy, in part because of the community's efforts to encourage citizens to "buy Waxahachie."

marking them as unworthy and incapable of taking care of themselves and their families. Men seemed particularly susceptible to such stigmatization (especially those who considered themselves fairly independent prior to the crash), and many hoped that the spring crop of 1933 would turn things around.

Waxahachie's cotton growers turned out a bumper crop that spring, but instead of salvation, the surplus proved a disaster for the county's 6,000 farmers. The families, already in massive debt from the previous years' declining commodity prices, found the market had completely collapsed. Cotton that had sold for 50¢ a pound in 1919 was going for 5¢ in 1933.

While the newspaper headlined such thoughts as "help of the kind in mind (direct relief) is an individual, a community, or a social obligation. It does not belong to a government founded for an entirely different purpose," Waxahachie's farmers had few options and thankfully turned to Roosevelt's proposed governmental programs for help.

In the spring of 1933, Ellis County's farmers turned for the first time to the federal government for relief. FDR had enacted the Agricultural Adjustment Act (AAA) to achieve parity; in other words, to return agricultural commodity prices to World War I levels. The unusually large cotton crop of 1933, added to an existing surplus, would increase world supplies to an unprecedented level—making cotton virtually worthless. To combat the impending disaster, the government

Although cotton prices plummeted during the 1930s, area farmers continued to grow the fiber that had previously brought so much wealth to the county. Farmers posed for a photograph in front of one of the many cooperative gins that operated in Ellis County during the 1930s and 1940s.

Land owners and their tenants often worked together to bring in the harvest. As late as the 1930s, farmers combined mechanization with their old trusty mules to bring in the crops.

determined to eliminate 10 million acres or 3 million bales of cotton by plowing the growing crop under. Offering an incentive of $11 an acre, the county's farmers eagerly complied with the government's plan. Local growers plowed up around 40 percent of the entire cotton crop in 1933. Every single farmer in the county participated in the program, much to the chagrin of cotton brokers, who claimed that farmers would never agree to plowing up their crop. Local farmers received more than $840,000 for their participation that spring.

Already looking to the next year, the AAA signed farmers up for the years ahead, farmers pledging to cut back their crop acreage for the receipt of payment checks. The following year, the federal government signed 865 cotton option checks worth over $275,000 to Ellis County growers, men who made an exacting distinction between the AAA program and the dole. Roosevelt's agricultural programs were voluntary, and farmers believed that they were making smart business decisions about their land, decisions that they made themselves for their families.

Thousands of farmers across the nation benefited from the AAA programs, but one group actually found that the programs spelled even greater economic disaster. Tenants and sharecroppers, always living marginal lives, could theoretically claim plow-up and cut-back checks from the federal government, but what proved possible in theory did not in reality. Faced with taking part of their land out of production, landowners turned their tenants off the land and simply did not plant the acreage that they had previously rented out, an unfair situation that the government had not predicted.

Although the number of tenant farmers declined dramatically in Ellis County during the Great Depression, African Americans still made up the largest number of these renting farmers and still did most of the heaviest labor. Notice the large brimmed hats worn by the men to protect themselves from the hot Texas sun.

In Ellis County, more than half of the farming population worked as tenants or sharecroppers. Estimates suggest that there were 5,263 white and 2,256 black families farming on the shares in 1930. Living in makeshift cabins with newspapered walls, these people already led subsistence existences—their diets consisting mainly of fat meat, cornmeal, and molasses—and during the Depression, even this was not affordable. Giving up on farming, more than half of the county's tenants left the blackland prairies during the decade, heading to bigger cities hoping to find work in one of Roosevelt's other federal programs.

But even smaller cities like Waxahachie benefited from the multitude of New Deal programs. The Reconstruction Finance Corporation (RFC) was one of the first non-agricultural programs to be enacted in the county. Functioning under a federal emergency relief law, the state allocated funds to individual cities to be distributed through their chambers of commerce. Ellis County received more than $17,000 from the RFC in the spring of 1933. More than 2,400 individuals applied for aid—51 percent of whom were white, 46 percent black, and 3 percent Hispanic. The money was allocated for wages and men were hired to improve cemeteries, work on county roads, clean up the sewer system, and refurbish schools. Eventually, 2,700 families in the county received aid from the RFC. Writing about the check recipients, a local newspaperman said, "a few of these people are not able to work because of a lack of food. There are many cases of pellagra, a direct result of not having enough food or an improper diet."

Poverty had become a major problem in Waxahachie, as it had throughout the United States, and many health related concerns were linked to a lack of money. Typhoid became the city's greatest health scare and the disease began to be diagnosed in alarming numbers. One family was known to have contracted the disease from eating food out of garbage cans from behind a restaurant on the downtown square.

Seeking greater relief, Waxahachians continued to look to the federal government for aid. The Public Works Administration, created to prime the economy by providing employment, granted the city $18,000 for school modernization—money to be spent on wages while the city provided funds for materials. Another program, the National Youth Administration, hired teenagers (thus removing them from the job market). In Waxahachie, the NYA improved the tennis and croquet courts in Getzendaner Park and built two new baseball diamonds: one at Trinity University and the other on the grounds of the cotton mill. The Works Progress Administration came to Waxahachie, too. The program employed over 100 men, "relieving the acute unemployment," and paid them to gravel dirt streets, repair the city's incinerator, and mark street names on curbs.

While these New Deal programs relieved some of the distress, the relocation of a Civilian Conservation Corps (CCC) camp in Waxahachie may have been

Roosevelt's many agricultural programs impacted Ellis County. This photograph of a farm demonstration on the Elgin K. Ward farm outside of Midlothian shows one of the many conservation techniques taught to the county's farmers.

the most significant in terms of long-range improvements of the governmental organizations to function in the county during the Depression. In late 1934, the chamber of commerce began putting together a bid for a CCC unit and contacted Senator Tom Connally and Representative Lyndon Johnson for help. By early 1935, Waxahachie had been chosen as the newest site for a soil erosion camp. Planning to open in April, estimates projected that the camp would be worth $500,000 to local farmers.

President Roosevelt designed the Civilian Conservation Corps to provide work relief to young men aged 18 to 25 and remove them from the job market. Over the next few years, nearly 3 million young men took to the land to work a variety of jobs in forests, parks, recreational areas, and soil conservation projects for $30 a month. Directed by army officers and foresters, the men worked under semi-military discipline.

The camp that eventually came to Waxahachie was first established at Fort Sam Houston in May 1933. Located in Clifton, the young men built a park on the Bosque River. After its completion, the camp moved to Belton where they began to work in soil conservation. Building miles of terracing and 1,500 concrete and rock dams, the men began the process of controlling the drainage of more than 9,000 acres of Bell County land.

Hoping to provide a similar service to Ellis County, the camp relocated in July 1935 to Waxahachie. Between 200 and 250 men worked at the camp,

The Civilian Conservation Corps camp in Waxahachie trained young men in the art of soil conservation. Their efforts during the 1930s assured fertile soil for future Ellis County farmers, many of whom continue to grow cotton today.

Waxahachie's downtown square continued to be the central trading and commercial hub of the region throughout the 1930s. Shoppers mingled with businessmen and court officials.

positioned on land donated by Dr. D.G. Thompson a few miles southwest of the courthouse (currently where FM 1446 crosses Interstate 35). An early contingent built 48 buildings: 40 small 6-man barracks, a mess hall, kitchen, recreational hall, infirmary, health and supply headquarters, office quarters, and a bathhouse. The recreation hall was equipped with chairs, a pool table, a ping-pong table, dominoes, and a radio. The hall also contained the camp library, or reading room as some of the men called it. The room was walled with plywood, varnished, and filled with bookshelves. In addition to comfortable chairs, the men supplied the library with books, magazines, and newspapers.

While offering the men a chance for work and travel, CCC programs promised to be wholesome places where good fun and leisure mixed with work in a directed atmosphere. The recreation hall, with its activities and library, fulfilled the camp's multiple purpose. The library, in addition to a quiet place to retire and relax, was also the site of the camp's educational programs where instructors, often army personnel, offered classes in such topics as typing, current history, wood working, reading, arithmetic, photography, first aid, safety driving, and music.

These educational classes helped fulfill another of the CCC's missions: to make the young men more employable when they left government service.

Bugs Tate, son of a local sharecropper, posed for this photograph in the 1920s. Tenant and sharecrop farming reached its peak in Waxahachie in the 1920s and then steadily declined, largely as a result of the Great Depression.

Locally, Trinity University offered 50 boys scholarships to study at the college while they were working for the CCC. Of these, one of the young men went on to complete a degree at Texas Agricultural and Mechanical College (now Texas A&M University), won a trip to Europe for his outstanding agricultural research, and was employed as a surveyor with the soil conservation service.

Although these various classes and programs helped the young men in many ways, the CCC helped Ellis County even more. The men constructed 319 miles of fencing and sodded 4,166 acres of pastureland. Converting 17,007 acres to strip cropping, the men made great strides at bringing the soil back into fertility. To control run-off and soil erosion, the men of the CCC terraced 3,025 acres and put an additional 17,651 acres into contour cultivation. They then reshaped and built a large retention dam along Waxahachie Creek, and built small ponds and reservoirs across the county to trap spring rains. In May 1937, the camp hosted two days of demonstrations geared toward soil conservation, a conference attended by more than 1,000 farmers.

The CCC left its mark on Waxahachie. The small ponds and water entrapments can still be seen today, dotting the county and providing watering holes for cows. Miles of terracing criss-cross former farmland, reminding the land's owners of their past occupants and the county's commitment to protect and nourish its soil.

As positive as programs like the Civilian Conservation Corps proved to be, they simply did not end the Great Depression. Although they provided some relief and certainly bolstered the emotional agony that many Americans suffered, they proved inadequate in the face of such tragedy. By the time the Japanese bombed Pearl Harbor in December 1942, Waxahachie had fundamentally changed.

Overwhelmingly committed to agriculture in 1930, 10 years later there were 400 less farms in the county, and the value of farm property had dropped by 42 percent. Crops, once valued at $12 million, had fallen to less than $6 million, and cotton, the basis of the community's economy, had plummeted from $10 million (already a figure much lower than growers had experienced throughout the early part of the century) to $4 million. The unemployment rate in the county jumped from 6.9 percent to 16 percent during the same 10 years, and consistently more than 2,000 people remained unemployed in the county, despite local New Deal programs hiring, at times, up to 3,500 men and women. In total, Ellis County received an estimated $3 million in federal relief funds, an amount equal to what other similarly sized Texas counties received.

Although there were few Waxahachians who did not feel the impact of the Great Depression, the city's citizens continually tried to maintain their morale and positive outlook on life. Movie theaters provided one cheap means of entertaining the local people while bolstering their self-esteem. Like Americans everywhere, Waxahachians became infatuated with Hollywood during the period and sought to escape reality in the movies. Throughout the 1930s, between 60 and 75 million people (nearly two-thirds of the nation) scrounged up enough dimes to fill theaters every week. Two theatres operated in Waxahachie during the Depression—the Empire and the Ritz—and both charged an average of 25¢ to see a motion picture.

Local boy Charlie Huff left Waxahachie and tried to make it in Hollywood during the Depression. Not successful, Huff returned to his native town and opened a dance studio.

Waxahachians, worn down by the Depression, sought solace in the town's two movie theaters. The Empire and the Ritz thrilled audiences with musical cowboys, leading men, and lovely ladies.

Movies tended to blend nostalgia for the lost Golden Twenties with the hope that renewed prosperity lay just around the corner. Musicals were especially popular and local citizens often saw pictures like *Forty-Second Street* and *Gold Digger*, movies that dealt with a variation on the old rags-to-riches story, two or three times. Actors like James Cagney, Charlie Chan, and Shirley Temple pulled in the old and young alike, and when Gene Autry, the "singing cowboy," made a personal appearance at the Ritz in 1937 to promote one of his movies, many stores shut down so that the owners might have a chance at seeing the Oklahoman sing "That Silver-Haired Daddy of Mine."

Swimming, long a favorite pastime of local residents, continued to be another inexpensive source of entertainment during the Depression years. Local entrepreneur S.W. Gough purchased some land and a cooling vat previously owned by the Texas Oil Products Company and opened the Crystal Plunge swimming hole in 1932. The vat measured 100 feet by 130 feet and measured 8 feet at its deepest point. Gough drained the pool every three weeks and cleaned the surface and then piped in fresh water from nearby Katy Lake (now the lake at the country club) through a 6-inch pipe.

Located only a half-mile off Grand Avenue, the swimming hole was easily accessible and cost 25¢ for a swim or seven swims for $1. Locals could purchase a season pass for $5 that entitled the holder to swim for the entire summer, a great bargain, especially since the pool was open from 7 a.m. until 10 p.m. The plunge featured a bath house at one end and spotlights on each corner. Two diving boards (one high and one low), a swing that extended over the pool, and a diving platform made of wood and pipes provided greater entertainment, and, if that was not enough, Gough hired the high school band to play on Friday nights.

The Crystal Plunge operated profitably for four years until late 1936 when an area boy drowned in the pool. Finding a basket of clothes at the day's end, pool operators went diving for the boy, but found nothing. The next day, the fire department drained the pool and brought up the boy's body. The Plunge closed for the season after the child's death and a serious drought in 1937 prevented its reopening.

Despite attempts to maintain morale, the Great Depression signaled an end to Waxahachie's most prosperous period. Along with the decreased demand for cotton, the local gins, compresses, and textile mill closed, putting a stranglehold on the county's entire economic base. In later years when cotton prices stabilized once again, local farmers found they could no longer compete. South and west Texas, thanks to advances in irrigation technology, had begun to grow large quantities of cotton, and Waxahachie forever lost its dominant position as the nation's largest and most significant cotton center.

Perhaps local people did not notice the passing of "King Cotton." After all, they were in the midst of the greatest depression the industrialized world had ever known when a second world war erupted. Throughout the 1930s, national newspapers related the storm brewing in Europe—the rise of Hitler in Germany and Mussolini in Italy, the Civil War in Spain, and the militarization of Japan—but the United States ignored the warnings, returning to a state of

Carlisle Chevrolet opened in 1926 and struggled to stay in business during the Depression years when car sales drastically fell off. The car attendants pictured would fill your car with gas, check your oil, and clean your windshield while you remained in the comfort of your automobile's cab.

isolationism after World War I and choosing to deal with internal difficulties rather than international affairs.

Most Americans hoped to avoid becoming entangled with European problems. Declaring itself neutral once again, as it had in World War I, the United States watched as Hitler's Germany forced the *Anschluss* (union) with Austria and rolled through the Sudeten territory and Czechoslovakia. As the crisis deepened, Britain and France pledged to protect Poland if Hitler attacked the country, which he did in September 1939. The world was at war once again just 20 years after the "war to end all wars" had ended.

Between 1939 and 1941, the United States vacillated in its international position. Shocked when France fell to Germany and sympathetic for the courageous British who held out against all odds, most Americans remained isolationist, hoping that two oceans would insulate the country from the war.

Such hope proved naïve, but when war came, it struck from an unexpected corner. The people of Waxahachie were shocked when they learned that Japan had attacked an American military base. Although most of them had no idea where Pearl Harbor was located, it was enough that it was United States soil.

Two local men who had joined the navy at the war's outset were stationed in Hawaii, and the newspaper asked citizens to pray for their safety and for the lives of all the American men trapped on the sinking ships. Although reluctant to enter the war, once the fight had been brought to the United States, Americans threw themselves into the effort—as one of Waxahachie's older citizens declared, "the Japs and the Nazis will find it a fight to the finish."

Local men began to volunteer immediately, joining others who had gone into the service prior to the country's official war declaration. Men like John Hiram Adair, who served as a tail gunner on a B-17 and was shot down over Italy, or James T. Kay, who was a mechanic on P-38 and P-51 planes in England and Germany.

The list of Ellis County volunteers continued to grow through the four years of war. Men and women joined the armed forces in large numbers—fighting in Europe and the Pacific. Daily, the local newspapers saluted the fighting soldiers, listing dead, wounded, and missing in action—a number that totaled 15 as early as 8 months into the war.

Enlisting was not the only means of forwarding the war effort, and Waxahachie turned its full attention to helping its men and women overseas. The government's War Production Board began the process of mobilizing the entire economy for the fight. Although Ellis County did not have the kind of industrial base needed to

The Gulf Filling Station volunteered as a scrap rubber collection point during World War II. The old tires stacked up were shipped to larger cities like Grand Prairie and then converted for use during the war.

convert facilities into war-making factories, the area did receive a few war supply contracts, which the citizens filled with eagerness, knowing that they were doing their part.

More often, local people participated in one of the government's many war programs. For example, Waxahachie consistently exceeded its war-bond goals, financing World War II's huge cost through citizen-lent money and taxes. Agreeing with President Roosevelt, the people believed that they would rather "pay one hundred percent of taxes now than push the burden of this war onto the shoulders of my grandchildren." Purchasing bonds and stamps faithfully, the community collected more than $1 million by the war's close. To keep up people's interest, collectors found new and exciting ways to tempt buyers. In August 1943, Waxahachie promoted "Buy a Bond and Drive a Jeep" Day. Every child that purchased $1 worth of war stamps received a ride around the square in an army Jeep, an exciting prospect considering that the Jeep had only recently been invented and remained exclusively a military vehicle.

In addition to the War Bond drives, Waxahachians participated in the Victory for Food Programs. Town folks converted their flowerbeds and empty lots into gardens and grew their own vegetables. The more ambitious attempted to can their tomatoes, cucumbers, and other foodstuffs, increasing their supply and

Despite the decreased crime rate during the war years, Waxahachie's police department continued to patrol the streets. The organization, along with a voluntary fire department, had been created during the late nineteenth century.

A soldier waits in front of the Gulf station for the bus. With rubber and gas shortages forestalling the use of personal vehicles, most travel during this period was undertaken via public transportation.

freeing up food for the military. Local farmers plowed up their old cotton fields, planting wheat, oat, rye, and sweet potatoes instead, selling their products directly to the government.

Along with the Victory for Food Program, Waxahachie participated in several other war drives. Housewives were asked to save their tin cans and deliver them to a nearby Coca-Cola bottling plant where they would be crushed and eventually converted to a war-time product. The city was recognized as collecting more grease in the "fats salvage" drive than any other community in the southwest. As the newspaper explained to readers, "a tablespoon of used waste fats saved each day by every housewife in America could be converted into a sufficiently large quantity of high explosives to dynamite axis armies from the face of the earth."

Even children got involved in the effort to win the war. Many saved pennies to purchase war stamps and collected tin during scrap metal drives. The Ritz Theatre ran a promotion encouraging the town's children to collect scrap rubber in 1942. Any child that brought at least one-quarter of a pound of scrap rubber to The Ritz was admitted free to a matinee during the drive. Announced in the newspaper, the Ritz's manager asked parents to encourage their children to gather between 1 pound and 4 pounds of scrap rubber.

Although thousands of miles from the fields of battle, Waxahachians on the homefront never forgot that the war was going on. Working to further the cause in every way, the city contributed on multiple levels. Staying abreast of the fighting—local leaders alerted the town to news by blasting whistles and sirens, sometimes firing notifications during the middle of the night. Such a warning fired at 4:00 in the morning on June 6, 1944. Although citizens had known that the long-awaited overland invasion of France would soon begin, they were still taken by surprise when the alarms began to blast, notifying them that their boys had crossed the English Channel and were landing on the beaches of Normandy. Turning on their radios, the town listened as the army relayed updates of the fighting.

Prayers were muttered throughout the remaining hours of the night, and many people dressed and gathered in the city's churches, coming together to ask God for his help and guidance, and for the safe delivery of their local men and women and all the forces who fought that day against the enemy. Leslie Rippey was one of the boys they prayed for that night. Rippey married Katie Bell, a local girl, and had volunteered in March 1941. Serving as a 10-millimeter mortar gunner and squad leader for the 1866th Service Command Unit, Rippey fought in Normandy and was wounded in the forearm.

There were dozens of other men like Rippey. Waxahachie native James Harry Hitt entered the army in 1942 and was assigned to the 19th Tank Battalion, 9th Armored Division. Sent to England, his division crossed the English Channel in October 1944, following the initial troops after the D-Day invasion, and began the long march to Luxembourg, Germany. Engaged in the Battle of the Ardennes (known popularly as the Battle of the Bulge), Hitt's company held the line in the vicinity of Echternach until late December when they marched 55 miles in bitter cold without sleep to begin a new attack along the Neufchateau-Bostogne Road in Belgium. With the Battle of the Bulge finally won, Hitt's company marched deeper into Germany, capturing the only remaining bridge across the Rhine River and encircling the Rurh Valley, trapping more than 300,000 German troops. Receiving new orders, Hitt marched toward the Elba River, 150 miles away, but was wounded during fighting, sustaining a fractured skull and total loss of hearing in his left ear. Serving his country faithfully, Waxahachie proudly acknowledged its native son's sacrifice in battle.

Although Hitt was wounded, he lived to return to his hometown. Other men were not so fortunate. Although an exact death toll is difficult to determine, at least 65 young Waxahachie men paid the ultimate sacrifice to preserve the democratic freedoms the United States enjoys, and 162 boys from Ellis County died as well. One of those men, Walter Windham, served in England, France, and Germany, and was killed in action in February 1945. Buried in Luxembourg, his family had his body exhumed and brought back to the blackland prairie where he was born.

Alice Longino dreaded war telegrams. Although she had supported the decision of each of her six sons to enlist and fight in the war, she knew that with that many boys fighting, the chances for injuries or death were great. But all six boys made it through the war unscathed—none of them were injured in any way—making Alice Longino one of the happiest mothers alive!

There were many mothers praying for their boys, but the "Good War," unlike the wars that had occurred before, had mothers also praying for their girls. For the first time, women were allowed to enlist in special sections of the armed

One of the many soldiers who fought in World War II, Paul Todd married local Waxahachie girl Sue Marie Barker. Both were employed by Gardenhire Department Store in Waxahachie before the war.

The Phillips Mechanical Training School opened in Waxahachie and trained several World War II veterans in mechanics.

forces—and they did. More than 300,000 young women served their country in an official capacity. One local woman, "Mickey" Ruby F. Tyler Hayes, entered the Women's Army Auxiliary Corps (WAAC) in 1943 and received her basic training in Georgia with several thousand other women. Having requested overseas duty, Hayes trained further at Fort Sill, Oklahoma, hiking 10 miles in full field packs, taking part in simulated air attacks, and rehearsing simulated ship abandonment. Receiving her orders, Hayes's company boarded the *SS Lurline*, which had been converted from a luxury liner to a troopship, and headed for Hollandia, New Guinea, in the Dutch East Indies.

The women spent 24 days aboard the *Lurline*, the first few green-faced and sick with seasickness. With the constant fear of mines and torpedoes, the women stayed alert all the time, wearing their life jackets all day just in case they were attacked. They received two meals a day—breakfast, consisting of boiled franks and boiled potatoes, and dinner, which had a little more variety. Finally reaching New Guinea, Hayes remained aware that an air attack was possible at any moment and a few of the WAACs were killed in a Japanese raid. Within a few months, Hayes was reassigned to Manila in the Philippines and served the remainder of the war in that city.

Waxahachie mourned with the rest of the country in April 1945 when President Franklin Roosevelt died, hosting a community memorial service at Central Presbyterian Church, and celebrated a month later when the victory in Europe was formalized. Sirens sounded once again, scaring a few of the older citizens, but soon the city's streets filled as people laughed and cried, hugging and kissing each other in joyful celebration that half the war had been won. The bulk of the community made its way downtown, gathering around the courthouse square and singing "The Star Spangled Banner." All the churches opened their doors, and many people spent time thanking God for the victory and praying for a speedy conclusion to the war. Later that night (May 8, 1945), the city held a formal thanksgiving service in the Getzendaner Park Auditorium, reflecting the religious views of the community.

Although Waxahachians celebrated the defeat of Hitler's Germany, they renewed themselves once again to continue the fight until Japan had surrendered "unconditionally." News had spread that the Japanese were suffering great losses, but had begun Kamikaze assaults, suicide missions where the pilots used their planes as weapons. One local boy stationed at Pearl Harbor wrote to his family, urging them not to let down now; "anyone back home who lets down on the job now, whether on a farm, a factory, a train or any of the essential jobs, will be guilty of helping to kill our boys."

Waxahachie did not let down its efforts. The community continued to work, raising money for the war effort and renewing its commitment to victory. Receiving word of the atomic bomb explosions and the destruction of Hiroshima and Nagasaki in August 1945, most Waxahachians thought little of the long-term consequences of the bombs and celebrated once again that an end to the war seemed in sight. The town gathered on the night of August 14, 1945 to celebrate Victory over Japan (V-J) Day. Encircling the courthouse square, the people prayed and sang together, offering a final thanksgiving to God that the war had ended and the Allies had emerged victorious.

Two tumultuous decades drew to a close. National issues had played out on the local level. Decisions made far beyond the Texas prairie had huge repercussions on people's lives, and they somehow had met the difficulties and risen to the challenge. Although greatly changed, Waxahachie emerged from the onslaught with renewed hope and optimism. The people of the community looked to their past success and knew that, through hard work, they could regain their city's place of prominence. The post-war years remained hard, but the city looked to truly diversify its economy. Although farming remained a mainstay, local leaders encouraged a variety of manufacturing facilities and began to look at other options for advertising their city.

7. A "Place in the Heart"

Eugene McMichael looked up from his work. The new shingles he was laying were starting to heat up. "Another typical Texas summer day," he thought, with temperatures expected to reach the mid-90s. Glancing across the roof's ridgeline, McMichael looked out across rows of new houses—many of which he had built during the past year—south toward the courthouse. The massive structure could still be seen, anchoring the older downtown section of Waxahachie, but new subdivisions were being created, almost daily stretching the city's limits further and further out from its central core. "Dad, are you out of nails?" Ronny called out, McMichael's younger son and helper during summer school breaks. "No," the older man replied, "just looking."

Gene McMichael, as he was known to family and friends, was one of the many builders in Waxahachie in the 1950s and early 1960s, helping to meet the post–World War II demand for housing. As hundreds of thousands of soldiers were demobilized, they longed to settle down, marry their sweethearts, buy a little house with a yard, and start families. Housing shortages quickly escalated and towns like Waxahachie worked rapidly to meet the demand. Aided by the federal government, soldiers received loans under the Servicemen's Readjustment Act of 1944 (known as the GI Bill of Rights) to build homes of their own. McMichael, a World War II veteran himself, worked to meet the shortage, sometimes framing up houses near the large Victorian homes of the previous century, but more often than not, sinking down piers in the waxy soil of new housing divisions.

Carving residential areas out of old farmland, the numerous subdivisions reflected a trend that continues to this day. Although farming remained a vital part of Ellis County's economy, the city began to encourage an industrial base. The population swelled as manufacturing plants required workers, which in turn encouraged new businesses to come to town to meet the increased demand for consumer goods. At first attracting working-class dwellers, by the 1980s Waxahachie had become known as a "bedroom community" to Dallas and Fort Worth, and hundreds of wealthy white-collar workers moved out of the metroplex to the quiet town, commuting each day to work.

At the end of World War II, the people of Waxahachie looked to reclaim their lives. Having lived through the Depression and the "great war," most hoped that the United States's booming economy would continue, and they looked forward to a happier future and a return to a more "normal" existence.

In Waxahachie, that meant a return to baseball. Always the town's favorite past-time, local leaders created the Ellis County Amateur League, a division comparable with Class A professional leagues. The young men, many of whom had fought in World War II and/or Korea, played for pay, fun, and the hope that they might make it to the "big leagues."

Not an unrealistic dream. Several of Waxahachie's players had seen action as Major League players. Charles Rabe played on the 1950 high school team and led the Indians (the high school's mascot) to the state championship. Losing at the state finals, the boys went on to win the state championship in the American Legion League. The Cincinnati Reds drafted Rabe and he joined Paul Richards, the town's most famous ball player, in the Majors.

Although Paul Richards was no longer a player by the 1950s—he was the general manager of the Baltimore Orioles—he remained the idol of many of Waxahachie's young ball players. Old-timers claimed that he was so good that the high school coach pulled him up as an eighth grader to play on the varsity team in the state championship tournament in 1921. His team lost that year, but they went

Waxahachie's high school baseball team lost the state playoffs in 1950, but went on to win the American Legion League playoffs. One of the players, Charles Rabe, went on to play in the major leagues.

This photograph shows the construction of a filling station on Elm Street. The increasing number of automobiles in Waxahachie proved one of the most significant changes in the city in the post–World War II years.

on to win the playoffs the next three years, years that made Richards a household name among Ellis County's young boys. Every kid around had a Paul Richards story; for example, it was common knowledge that he had once pitched the first game of a double-header with his right arm and then pitched the second with his left.

True or not, after graduating from Waxahachie High School in 1926, Richards went on to dazzle fans in several Major League towns. Playing outstanding ball on the 1933 World Series Champion New York Giants, Richards beat his own record when he hit two doubles and knocked in the winning run of the seventh game for the Detroit Tigers in the 1945 World Series.

The reemergence of baseball as a prime pastime in Waxahachie helped to ease the city back into a normal routine. Although life around the Texas town would never be the same, the people fell into a rhythm and continued to pull together as a community.

The city's population had continued to increase: 12,500 people lived within the city limits in 1947. The more socially elite met weekly at the new country club, built west of downtown on a lake originally created by one of the railroads that ran through town, for a round of golf or dinner in the clubhouse. Two airports serviced the area and a large sanitarium provided medical care.

Trinity University, originally relocated to the city in 1901, closed its doors in 1944, believing that a move to a larger city would help to boost its sagging student population (the university reopened in San Antonio where it now continues to provide students a fine liberal arts education). Moving into the vacated buildings, Southwestern Bible Institute began operating the same year, attracting students with the promise of educating them within the doctrine of the Assembly of God church. Within a few years, the school changed its name to Southwestern Assembly of God University and continues to this day to meet the higher educational needs of Texas students.

The increased use of automobiles marked one of the biggest changes in the city following the war. The old electric streetcars were dismantled and the interurban ceased to run. Waxahachians, like Americans everywhere, had fallen in love with their cars. Dealerships, particularly Carlisle's, which had operated since the 1920s, saw a brisk business as customers wanted the latest conveniences, including power windows and radios, for their Sunday afternoon drives. The county's commitment to paving all its roads helped to further the automobile craze.

Along with paved roads, Ellis County fully electrified itself. Although the electrification of the county's farms and remote areas had started during the Great Depression under the Rural Electrification Act (sponsored by Texas's own senator Lyndon B. Johnson), it was not until the 1950s that virtually all of the farms in Ellis County had electricity. With the new technology in place, many farm wives enjoyed a greater ease of living and looked to purchase more conveniences, like washing machines and vacuum cleaners.

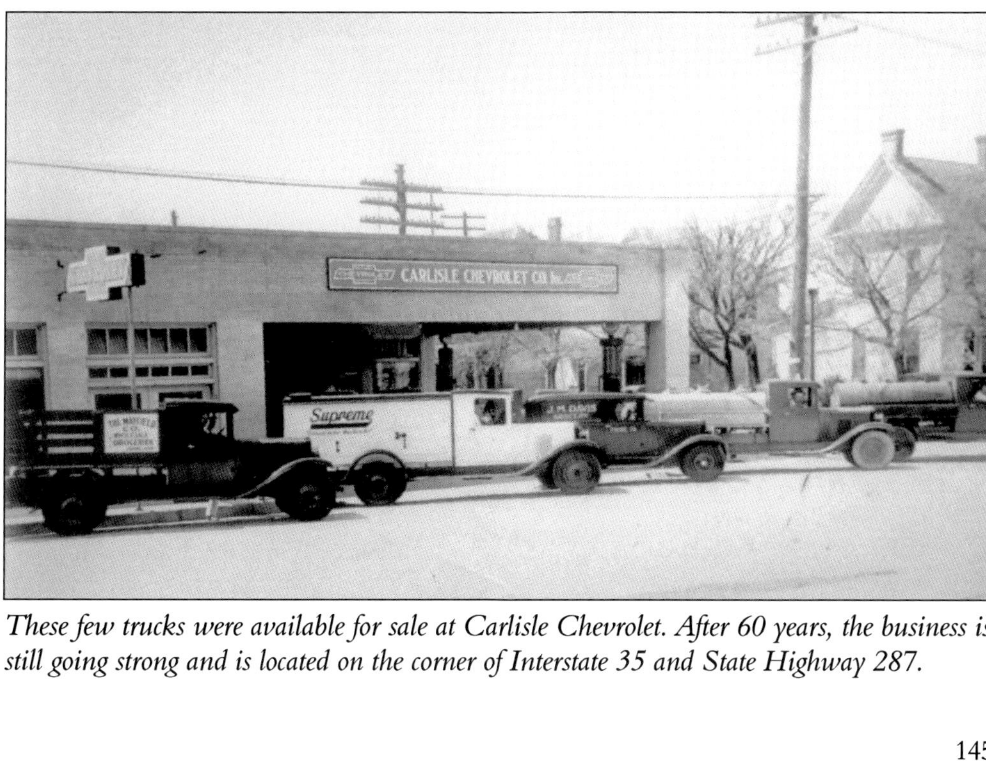

These few trucks were available for sale at Carlisle Chevrolet. After 60 years, the business is still going strong and is located on the corner of Interstate 35 and State Highway 287.

Such marvels dazzled the farm wives, many of whom had trudged through the Depression only to find themselves managing farms by themselves during the war. Some simply stopped farming and moved to Dallas, Arlington, or Fort Worth for the war's duration, finding jobs in defense plants. When their husbands returned from duty, they once again moved to their land, but many did not go back to the old ways. Instead of planting cotton, the men grew maize, wheat, and rye, an agricultural return to the greater diversification of pre–Civil War days. Additionally, many landowners completely stopped farming and converted their land to ranches, raising cattle or sheep.

Another significant change occurred in 1953 when oil was located in the county. Although it did not lead to any major "gushers," the discovery fueled a move to extract oil, and later natural gas, and led to the building of an oil refinery plant outside Waxahachie.

By the late 1950s, local leaders had shifted the county's economy toward manufacturing, encouraging the relocation and building of multiple factories. V.F. Armstrong Cork Company was one of the first manufacturing facilities to move to Waxahachie, and the plant produced 5,000 amber colored bottles a day for the brewing industry. There were also two garment factories, two furniture plants, one woodcraft shop, two venetian blind facilities, and two candy producers. One of the sweetest businesses functioning was Burleson and Sons Apiary, a honey distributor that gathered nectar locally and bottled the liquid gold for statewide sales. The city's industrial base continued to expand throughout the 1960s, and more industries moved to Waxahachie, including a large fiberglass plant and a wholesale nursery company.

Oil was discovered in the county in the early 1950s. An oil refinery plant was built outside of Waxahachie to refine the county's oil.

Waxahachie's oil refinery began servicing the region after oil was discovered in neighboring Corsicana in the 1950s. Struggling against pressure of damaging local wildlife and water reservoirs, the refinery closed down.

Many business leaders found Waxahachie attractive, including such non-profit groups as the Presbyterian Children's Home. Relocating to the city in 1960, the church purchased 277 acres of land along Interstate 35 to build a home for needy children. The church built six children's residences, living quarters for the "house parents," a clinic and staff quarters, a laundry, and a recreational building. Waxahachie welcomed its newest citizens and eagerly helped the little ones move in.

The rapid growth experienced throughout the 1950s and 1960s slowed during the next decade, a reflection of national tensions resulting from the Vietnam War, presidential scandals involving Johnson and Nixon, and the inflation and oil crisis of Carter's administration. The community remained at a virtual standstill for ten years, but saw its economic prospects return once again during the 1980s.

Seeking to further diversify its economy, Waxahachie's leaders took an unprecedented step and sought to make the city the Hollywood of the southwest. The major motion picture *Bonnie and Clyde*, starring Faye Dunaway and Warren Beatty, had been filmed in the county in 1967. Its box office success encouraged city planners to speak with representatives of the film industry, asking them to consider further filming in the city. Several major movies were filmed in and around Waxahachie during the 1980s including *The Trip to Bountiful*, starring Dorothy Malone and Ed Nelson; *Tender Mercies*, starring Robert Duvall, Tess Harper, and Wilford Brimley; and *1918*, starring Matthew Broderick.

Places in the Heart was probably the most famous of the movies filmed in the city during this period. Nominated for several awards, the film, starring Sally Field, Danny Glover, and John Malkovich, tells the story of Edna, who is suddenly thrust into the role of family provider when her husband is accidentally killed by a drunken gunman. Trying to keep her family together, Edna agrees to plant cotton with "Mose," an out-of-work African-American man trying to scrape by in the Depression-era racist south. The two face terrible challenges, including a tornado and the Ku Klux Klan, attempting to bring the first bale of cotton into the gin to win the year's prize money. The movie portrays the Great Depression in Waxahachie in 1935, rendering a poignant story of life, love, and the barriers humans erect between themselves.

In addition to major motion pictures, at least a dozen made-for-television movies were made in or around Waxahachie during the 1980s. These include *Of Mice and Men*, *Cowboy*, and *The Last of the Caddoes*, and starred actors such as Randy Quaid, Robert Blake, and Ted Danson. Several television commercials were also filmed in the city—many of them airing in South America—and included products such as TU Electric, A-1 Mobile Homes, Kellogg's, Nabisco, Radio Shack, and Fiat.

Seemingly bursting with prosperity, Waxahachie's economy continued to boom. City leaders explored other, more non-traditional means of supplementing the town's economic bases. In 1989, Waxahachie was chosen by the United States Congress as the sight of the first Super Conducting Super Collider ever built

After World War II, Waxahachians attempted to pick up the pieces of their lives. Local events like this rodeo restored the community's sense of place. Charlie Huff, who had once owned a dance studio in town, had been elected county clerk and now played the fiddle at county events.

After World War II, Happy Drummond began selling hamburgers out of a little store front downtown. Drummond sold four burgers for a $1, and many of the town's youth would eat four at a time.

in the United States. The proposed 54-mile tunnel would accelerate electrically charged protons so that scientists might conduct collision experiments, leading to technological advances that several European countries were already developing. Excited by the potential possibilities, a commission was created that purchased more than 17,000 acres of land west of Waxahachie on which to construct the experimental research station. Construction companies hired by the thousands, creating new jobs for blue-collar workers and administrative assistants on a daily basis. Hundreds of scientists and engineers flooded into the county (creating another housing shortage and then building boom) and prepared to experiment.

Despite the eagerness of Waxahachie's citizens, the Super Conductor was destined for closure. After years of congressional squabbling, including claims that the project was just more "pork for Texas," the project was defunded. More than 14 miles of tunnel had already been constructed underground in addition to a magnet-development complex, a linear accelerator, and a central facility. At its peak, the Collider employed 2,100 local residents.

After the disaster of the Super Conducting Super Collider, business leaders looked for more locally controlled means of expanding the economy, mainly through tourism. Recognized as a leading historical community through the film exposure the city had received, Waxahachie joined the Texas Main Street Program, which was part of the Texas Historical Commission's Community Heritage Development Division and a branch of the Main Street National Trust. The program was designed to improve all aspects of the downtown business district, including economic management, the strengthening of public participation, recruiting new businesses, and rehabilitating the old structures. Building on downtown's inherent assets—rich architecture, personal service, traditional values, and a sense of place—the Main Street program rekindled entrepreneurship, downtown cooperation, and civic concern.

As part of the initial move to restore the city's architecturally important structures, local citizens banded together and raised funds to restore the Old Park Jail. Built in 1929, the structure is incredibly unique; known as a rotary jail, only four were ever built in the United States. The center of the building comprised a revolving cage surrounded by individual cells. The inner compartment was rotated by a crank, and the single entry to the main cage served as the door to each cell as the shaft was turned in a circular motion. Intended to decrease jailbreaks—several were reported to have escaped from the old county prison—the significant structure has been restored and is occasionally opened for tours.

In addition to revitalizing downtown, the city's involvement with the Main Street USA program spurred a movement to clean up Getzendaner Park. The changes included the creation of a jogging trail and new bridges across the creek that flows through the park, which complemented the prior restoration of the old Chautauqua auditorium. The city once again began to book cultural venues in the octagonal structure, many produced by the newly formed Community Theater group or the town's Symphony Association.

Following the move to restore the city's historically significant public buildings, many of Waxahachie's Victorian-era homeowners began to apply for state and national historical designations for their private homes. An estimated 267 markers now grace the city—more than any other town in Texas.

With many of the city's older homes designated as historic sites, homeowners became interested in restoring their residences to their former glory. The Williams house (412 West Marvin Street) was one of the first homes in the city to be extensively restored. Originally built in 1893 by grocery store owner Ed Williams for his new bride Ella, the house cost $6,400. Williams probably expected to pay the majority of its balance with money he had recently inherited after his father's death, but the cash ran out before the home was completed. Williams was forced to give mechanic's liens on the structure for the amounts he still owed to the lumberyard and his builder. Although there is little concrete evidence, Williams appears to have been a gambler (an Ed Williams appears three times in county records with gaming charges, and he was sued in civil court for bad debts). Whether unlucky in business or gambling, Williams sold the house he had built for his bride in 1902.

The Williams house has been lovingly restored and sports a pale pink exterior with white gingerbread trim. With a corbelled chimney, roof cresting, beveled corners with knee brackets, and a Moorish arched porch valence, the home is one of the city's best examples of the late Victorian style.

The Patrick House (233 Patrick Street) has been maintained for the last 100 years by the original family. Built in 1899 by Marshall T. Patrick for his wife and three unmarried daughters, the structure was based on a design published in *The Scientific American, Architects and Builders Edition*. A well established businessman, land developer, and banker, Patrick purchased a 10-acre plot of land in the West End Addition and built a house in the Queen Anne style with a prominent corner tower, asymmetrical façade, shingle siding, and steeply pitched roofs. The large imposing home also had slender, classical porch columns and a Palladian window in the third floor gable.

Although two of the daughters married, a third remained single and lived in the house until her death in 1969 at the age of 94. Since her death, descendents of Marshall Patrick have maintained the house and grounds, which includes all its original outbuildings, such as a barn, windmill house, servants' quarters, arbor, and underground hothouse.

In addition to private homes, several of the city's finer houses have been restored and opened to the public as bed and breakfast inns. These include the Harrison House, built in 1915 by James Wright Harrison and now ornamented

Local Waxahachie girl Jackie Faye Williams rode in one of Waxahachie's many street parades. The beauty queen was preparing to compete in the Miss Texas pageant.

with English country décor, and the Chaska House, built in 1900 and filled with period antiques lovingly collected by the innkeepers.

Recognizing the increased importance of tourism in the local economy, the chamber of commerce organized or supported several local festivals. For example, the chamber sponsors the Gingerbread Trail, a tour of some of the city's most well maintained and restored homes, that occurs the first weekend of June each year. Soon after its creation, other fetes were begun, including a candlelight tour of homes during the Christmas season; the Crepe Myrtle Festival on the Fourth of July, which includes fireworks and a free symphony concert; and Bethlehem Revisited.

Organized by the city's churches and held on the grounds of the Central Presbyterian Church, Bethlehem Revisited is a living history museum of the time of Christ's death. Painstakingly recreated, authentic structures house re-enactors who ply the foods and wares of the period. Craftspeople weave wool and tanners dry leather. Camels and sheep walk the streets with the crowds, adding realistic noises and smells. The crowds swell, especially as Joseph, pulling an obstinate mule with a pregnant Mary on board, walks toward the stable. The North Star shines over the couple and a menagerie of animals as the sleeping baby Jesus rests peacefully in his manger.

The Hosford-Streich Home, built in 1893, personified the "gingerbread" look so popular among Victorian homes built in the city before 1900.

One of the city's restored downtown buildings, the Ellis County Museum educates locals and visitors about the history of Waxahachie.

Though less theatrical, the Ellis County Museum, originally begun in the late 1960s, occupies a restored corner store across from the courthouse downtown. Its collections, ranging from a woman's decorative fan display to various grades of cotton bolls, educate the visitor and provide a visual history of the community. An affiliated organization, the Ellis County Art Museum attracts area residents, while eager art lovers can see the museum's display of a variety of paintings.

For art lovers with more eclectic tastes, the Webb Gallery on West Franklin Street offers one of the finest displays of national and regional self-taught artists in the United States. It also houses the Webb Photo Archive and Library, one of the most extensive and current collections of folk art ephemera in Texas.

Visitors looking to enrich their artistic experience of Waxahachie can visit the 1895 restored Texas Theater on the north side of the square. Bands, singers, and songwriters representing the best of the Texas music scene perform at the theater weekly.

With a population of more than 21,000 people, Waxahachie today represents a thriving city. With one eye on its future and the other on its past, the city has

Pioneer Nicholas P. Sims farmed some of Ellis County's best land. When he died, he donated his entire estate to the city to create a library. The Nicholas P. Sims Library, named in his honor, still serves the community's educational and literary needs today.

embraced the many changes it has encountered over the years. Expanding from a small pioneering community along a creek to an industrial center, the population has continually changed with the times.

The years between Reconstruction and the Great Depression earned Waxahachie the name of the queen city of the cotton belt. Poor but proud tenant farmers walked the same downtown streets as the city's wealthiest land and business owners, always in the shadow of the red sandstone courthouse that towers over the prairie landscape. Both groups believed that they would make it big with King Cotton.

That optimism propelled the county on to greater agricultural outputs than any other region in the nation. The banner "number one cotton producer in the world" hung proudly beneath the city's name on promotional brochures for years. Seemingly endless potential for wealth, coupled with the socially elegant life that accompanied it, made Waxahachie one of the most beautiful and envied cities in Texas.

World-class universities and public schools, the annual Chautauqua Assembly, and other educational facilities supported the city's rise to fame, but the abundant life was cut short by the Great Depression. Waxahachie struggled along during the years of crisis, emerging in the aftermath of World War II a very different city, but one that still displayed that early frontier spirit of community cooperation and success.

Earning a "place in the heart" of Texans everywhere, thousands now visit the city each year, enjoying the restored buildings and houses. Some eat in the many restaurants that grace downtown, places like the Dove's Nest that have earned statewide recognition for their interpretation of the New American Cuisine. Others stay in the restored Rogers Hotel—experiencing hotel life *c.* 1912 when cotton reigned king in Waxahachie.

For over 150 years, Waxahachie has reflected the diverse economic and social life of north-central Texans. From its boom period to the years of uncertainty, the city has survived and illustrated the same sort of enthusiasm that marked its earliest days. Were Wild Bill Cody and his troupe of actors to visit the city again, 100 years later, they would be greeted just as enthusiastically as they had been in October 1902. A city proud of its history, local people still gather downtown around the courthouse square, eagerly anticipating the excitement of the future, perhaps just around the corner of Rogers Street.

Men made weekly visits to the barbershop located in the basement of the Rogers Hotel. A cut, shave, and shine kept the local businessmen looking fine.

BIBLIOGRAPHY

PRIMARY SOURCES

Dallas *Morning News.*

Ellis County. "Ellis County Commissioner's Court Minutes, 1850." Courthouse Annex, Waxahachie.

Stoddard, Anne Frances Matthews. Memoir. Ellis County Museum, Waxahachie.

Texas Almanac and State Industrial Guide.

U.S. Bureau of the Census. *Fifteenth Census of the Population, 1930.*

U.S. Bureau of the Census. *Sixteenth Census of the Population, 1940.*

Vertical Files. Ellis County Museum, Waxahachie.

Vertical Files. Nicholas P. Sims Library, Waxahachie.

Waxahachie Chamber of Commerce. *Waxahachie, Texas, in 1922: An Ideal Home City*. Waxahachie: no publisher, 1922.

Waxahachie *Daily Light.*

Waxahachie *Enterprise.*

Winn, Birdie Farrar. *All Roads lead to Texas*. Dallas: PIP, 1968.

SECONDARY SOURCES

Addington, Wendall G. "Slave Insurrections in Texas." *Negro Journal of History* 35 (October 1950): 408-434.

Billingsley, John B. "A Trip to Texas." *Texana* 7 (1969): 201-219.

Britton, Karen G. *Bale o' Cotton: The Mechanical Art of Cotton Ginning*. College Station: Texas: Texas A&M University Press, 1992.

Citizens National Bank. *A History of Waxahachie, Texas, and Citizens National Bank*. Waxahachie: 1968.

Cobb, James C. and Michael V. Namorato. *The New Deal and the South*. Mississippi: University Press of Mississippi, 1984.

Culbertson, Margaret. *Texas Houses Built by the Book: The Use of Published Designs, 1850-1925*. College Station: Texas A&M Press, 1999.

Donnelly, Mary Louise. *St. Joseph's Catholic Community, Waxahachie, Texas: Our Parish's 125 Years, 1874-1999*. Ennis: M.L. Donnelly, 1999.

Dunn, Roy Sylvan. "The KGC in Texas." *Southwestern Historical Quarterly* 70 (April 1970): 367-398.

Ellis County Historical Museum and Art Gallery, Inc. *Ellis County History: The Basic 1892 Book with Additional Biographies*. Fort Worth: Historical Publishers, 1972.

Felty, Margaret Leslie Rowland. "Waxahachie: A Kaleidoscopic History, 1850–1900." Master's thesis, University of Texas at Arlington, 1975.

Hardy, Heck, Moore, and Inc. "Historical Resources of Waxahachie, Texas: A Comprehensive Survey and National Register of Historic Places Nomination." Austin, Texas: 1985.

Hazel, Michael V. "They called it Chautauqua." *Legacies* 8 (Spring 1996): 26-32.

Hawkins, Edna Davis et al. *History of Ellis County, Texas*. Waco, Texas: Library Binding Company, 1972.

Lewis, James David. "The Historical Development of Higher Education in Ellis County." Dissertation, University of North Texas, 1993.

Morrison, Theodore. *Chautauqua*. Chicago: University of Chicago Press, 1974.

Tyler, Ron et al., eds. *The New Handbook of Texas*. 6 vols. Austin: Texas State Historical Association, 1996.

Valek, Wesley. "Czech-Moravian Pioneers of Texas, 1874-1917. *Panhandle-Plains Historical Review* 56 (1983): 49-63.

INDEX

This photograph of an unidentified early family home in Waxahachie included the family's bird dog.